LET THE DAUGHTERS *Arise*
VOL. 2

DR. MONIQUE FLEMINGS

©Copyright 2021 Dr. Monique Flemings

All rights reserved. This book is protected under the copyright laws of the United States of America.

ISBN-13: 978-1-954609-16-7

No portion of this book may be reproduced, distributed, or transmitted in any form, including photocopying, recording, or other electronic or mechanical methods, without the written permission of the publisher, except in the case of brief quotations embodied in reviews and certain other non-commercial uses permitted by copyright law. Permission granted on request.

For information regarding special discounts for bulk purchases contact the Publisher:
LaBoo Publishing Enterprise, LLC
staff@laboopublishing.com
www.laboopublishing.com

All information is solely considered as the point of view of the authors.

Scripture quotations marked (NIV) are taken from the Holy Bible, New International Version®, NIV®. Copyright © 1973, 1978, 1984, 2011 by Biblica, Inc.™ Used by permission of Zondervan. All rights reserved worldwide. www.zondervan.com

Scripture quotations marked ESV are from the Holy Bible, English Standard Version, copyright © 2001 by Crossway Bibles, a publishing ministry of Good News Publishers. Used by permission. All rights reserved.

The Holy Bible, King James Version. Cambridge Edition: 1769; King James Bible Online, 2019. www.kingjamesbibleonline.org.

Scripture quotations marked (NLT) are taken from the Holy Bible, New Living Translation, copyright ©1996, 2004, 2015 by Tyndale House Foundation. Used by permission of Tyndale House Publishers, Inc., Carol Stream, Illinois 60188. All rights reserved.

Scripture quotations marked TPT are from The Passion Translation®. Copyright © 2017, 2018 by Passion & Fire Ministries, Inc. Used by permission. All rights reserved. ThePassionTranslation.com.

Zondervan Publishing House. The Amplified Bible (1965). Thirtieth printing, March 1985. Library of Congress Catalog Card Number 65-19500.

The Message (the Bible in contemporary language). 2005. Colorado Springs, CO: NavPress

TABLE OF CONTENTS

Introduction..1

It's Time to Handle Your Business Like a Queen! –
   Dr. Nakita Davis......................................5

You Must Remove The Dead Bodies! – Dr. Nikki Zeigler.....15

I'll Wait!!! – Brenda Carroll Lofton.....................21

Finding God in Darkness – Jalima Cook....................31

Helping Until it Hurts Learning to Carry my own Load –
   Pamela Kennedy.......................................43

Trauma In The Womb – Dyrell Lee..........................53

Surviving Beyond The Shame – Elder Sabrina Renee Penn....67

UnBeGrievAble! – Wenona Kelley...........................77

Stormy Weather – Tanya C. Young..........................85

7 Principles of Breakthrough – Dr. Carleta Alston........101

About The Visionary Author..............................115

INTRODUCTION

I stepped out of my bedroom and my eyes immediately fixed on this large, strange figure on my living room wall. It was odd, almost like wall art, but I don't have wall art. With my eyes fixed on this new wall art, I continued to take slow steps toward it and suddenly … it moved! It was a very large centipede and I spun around, ran up the stairs and locked myself in my bedroom. Terrified by this large bug, I called my parents and told them about the large centipede on the wall of my living room. My mother could hear the terror in my voice. My father was absolutely amazed that I called them. A very grown woman, in my own home, calling my parents who live about 45 minutes away to come and rescue me from the largest bug that I had ever seen in my life.

I was gripped with fear to the point that I left my home and drove to a store parking lot, where I waited for my parents to come. I sat in terror in my car waiting for them to approach my subdivision. Once they arrived, we entered my home and yes, by that time the large centipede was gone. My fears increased even more. I really wanted my mother to stay with me but by then my father was annoyed and not having any more of my personal meltdown. My parents left and I spent the night in my home, locked behind my bedroom door in a full anxiety attack. The largest bug that I had ever seen was in my home somewhere and I felt absolutely powerless.

It was after this incident that I realized that my fears were on the extreme side and that my life was really ruled by so many fears. I know that everyone has fears because it's a normal emotion, but my fears were on overdrive to the point that my life was governed by fear. The fact that a bug had the power to cause me to leave my home was incredible. I was paralyzed and gripped by fear but not just of bugs—I was fearful of so many things in life. I was fearful of new relationships. I was fearful of failure. I was a people-pleaser and I self-sabotaged and I devalued my voice.

I lived my life with a muzzle, and I functioned well. I interacted, established a career, served in ministry, all with a muzzle over my voice. So I was always shrinking back in fear that I would not be accepted or that my voice did not matter. It was a journey of silent pain behind the muzzle.

I began to do the work that was required to remove my muzzle and crush my fears. It was a process of unraveling years of fear-based thinking that was triggered by a fear that I did not want to face. As I slowly crushed my fears, I found my voice. I found my freedom and I found my authenticity. I dumped fake sister-friends, and like blinders removed from my eyes, I saw my authentic sister-friends that had been in my life and carrying me through life the entire time. I fell in love with the real me. Yes, the authentic me was a pretty dope woman. I actually loved who I was, and I was able to celebrate me…authentically.

I knew that other women had a similar journey and I felt compelled to do my part in loosing my sisters from their muzzles. *Let the Daughters Arise Volume II* is a collaboration of powerful stories of victory and triumph from women who thought their voices were not significant. The *Let the Daughters Arise* inaugural book

Introduction

exploded with life-changing stories from some amazing co-authors who poured their pain on the pages of a book to create a legacy. We have continued this same legacy in *Let the Daughters Arise Volume II*. The torch has been passed and the legacy continues.

You will find yourself in these pages and you will reach back for this book over and over for insight and wisdom. Each story is a life lesson full of encouragement, empowerment, and strategies. We are just getting started. *Let the Daughters Arise* is more than a book. It's a movement. It's a freedom movement to provide an environment where women can heal, share their story, and launch a business. Women's entrepreneurship is a necessity. The voices of women will no longer remain silent under pain and dismissal. The voices of women will not be muzzled, and their genius taken to the grave. The voices of women are full of joy and strength, and together we are creating a legacy.

Thank you for trusting me and these amazing authors to come into your life and share our wisdom. You will not be disappointed. Now, I present to you an amazing work...*Let the Daughters Arise Volume II*...ENJOY!

Dr. Monique Flemings
Visionary Author
Monique Flemings Enterprises

Dr. Nakita Davis is an Award-Winning Publisher, PR Maven, Global Influencer, and Public Figure with an unshakable Faith and passion to see Women Win in Christ! She is a Proud For(bes) the Culture official member, a 2x Presidential Volunteer Service Award-Winner under President Barack Obama, an ATT Dream in Black Future-Maker honoree, and was named Top 100 Successful Women in Business by the GTC of Commerce in South Florida.

She is the CEO of **Jesus Coffee and Prayer Christian Publishing House LLC,** and has helped hundreds of Women to Live Out Their God-Sized Dreams of Authorship and gained National visibility through her robust Publishing and PR platform. Dr. Davis collaborations/media sponsorships and connections have resulted in her/her clients being Nationally recognized on FOX, NBC, CBS, BET, People magazine, Blavity, SHEEN, Los Angles Tribune, Tamron Hall Show, The View, Disrupt magazine, Stellar Awards, the Gospel Billboard Top 100 Charts, Grammy and Superbowl Billboards too. She owns the **Women Win Network,** a Television Network and Magazine company celebrating Women Who Win 365!

Her Motto: Queen, It's Time to Play Your Royal Position!

Dr. Davis is an Ordained Minister and lives with her loving husband and two beautiful children in Atlanta, GA. Follow on IG @jesuscoffeeandprayer & @womenwinnetwork

IT'S TIME TO HANDLE YOUR BUSINESS LIKE A QUEEN!

Dr. Nakita Davis

Queen, it's time to play your royal position!

I have probably said this phrase literally a million times, if not more. Outside of Christ being the anchor for my soul and God being my foundation, this statement has been impressed upon the very fabric of **who** I know God has called me to be. More importantly, it is the very challenge in which I encourage my fellow Sisters in Christ and business to rise above the noise and distraction that the enemy desperately uses to keep their assignment stuck, stagnant, and stale.

It is more than a *cute* catch phrase or a trendy post for Instagram or twitter. It is a call for every Woman who is a believer in Christ to **'handle her business like a queen!'**

The days of sitting on your high horse, looking cute, prim and proper, but unwilling to do the real work required to lead your people to victory, are OVER!

The best biblical correlation that God gave me as a guiding roadmap draws from the book of ***Esther***. In essence, she was a beautiful orphan girl who rose to power as Queen with the help of her beloved cousin Mordecai. This journey, just like our lives, did not come without hiccups and adversity. There came a time when Queen Esther had to rise above and stop playing small—even as Queen—so she could save the lives of her beloved Jewish people and ultimately herself.

Esther originally did not want to rock the boat when she was asked to speak with her husband and plead for deliverance for her people. Her first human inclination was fear and an excuse (Esther 4:11).

But thanks be to God, her cousin Mordecai, through relentless pursuit, obedience, and instruction, was able to persuade Esther to ***play her royal position!***

The muzzle was off.

In my personal, professional, business, and spiritual journey there have been several opportunities in which I could have played it safe, taken the easy road, and the path most frequently traveled like the rest. Unfortunately for the devil, that is just not who God created me to be!

Just like Queen Esther, I was created for a time such as this.

As a daughter of the Most-High King, it was time for me to arise like never before in late Winter of 2019. I remember it like it was yesterday. My husband and I had already determined that we needed a change of scenery. We both were born and raised in Charlotte, North Carolina, and it would forever be our home, but we knew God had called us to more.

At the end of 2018, in prayer, full agreement and unison, we declared that Atlanta, Georgia would be our new home in 2019. We declared boldly—specifically—that it would be our Land of Milk and Honey. In faith, I put in the transfer with my Fortune Top 9 organization to move to Atlanta. We didn't know how long the process would be or if an immediate opportunity would come, but we trusted God by faith that it would. And it did.

Not only did an opportunity come, but it came within two months and an offer was extended to me on my birthday in February. By March of 2019, I had accepted the career move to Atlanta. We were excited, but also had never experienced such a swift change and all the stress associated with juggling our home in Charlotte with two kids and me (mommy) traveling back and forth every week to Atlanta. It was insane, to say the least.

I was used to traveling for work, as I was in leadership and sales, but back-to-back for 12 weeks was an entirely different stress level. It took approximately three months to juggle a brand-new team, a new boss, new systems, a new environment, crazy traffic (did I say CRAZY traffic)—all while truly becoming a Proverbs 31 woman. On lunch breaks I was meeting with my real estate agent, trying to find the perfect house for my family to live, researching school systems appropriate for my tween daughter, and still striving to operate my GROWING BUSINESS: Jesus, Coffee, and Prayer Christian Publishing House, LLC.

This was the very purpose of moving to Atlanta in the first place. Toss in the unfortunate sabotage of women who looked just like me while I was trying to get my family settled from out of state and there were moments that I could not *breathe*—not in the literal sense, but certainly metaphorically speaking.

I couldn't wrap my head around this being the path that God had called me to when it felt like every turn was a problem. Every path appeared to be a hiccup. Every snare was out, and I could feel Satan on my heels.

All I wanted to do was be obedient to the calling over my life.
All I wanted to do was make an impact pleasing to God.
All I wanted to do was build a legacy for my family and my kids' kids.

I remember thinking, *Lord, why is this so hard?* I also remember thinking, *Lord, you promised that you would never leave me nor forsake me! I know you won't put more on me than I can bear.*

God hears your cry, and He cares for you.

Fast-Forward

When we moved to Atlanta, the original game plan was to still work the 9-5 for 18 months, build Jesus, Coffee, and Prayer on the side and then take the full leap of faith. Our hope was to save some money and be in a better position to go into full-time entrepreneurship with both our endeavors.

But God.

Because, I was a willing vessel, obedient, and stepped out on faith when God said so, He literally accelerated our timeline right before our eyes.

We closed on the house within three months of 2019. In the next six months, God had positioned me to put in my exit notice with my company of nearly 15 years of corporate leadership and sales on my OWN accord. I was not fired, downsized, or let go. I left with an impeccable record of excellence and still remain in great regard with many of the leadership until this very day. I became a full-time entrepreneur on December 31, 2019—Glory to God.

Watch this:

God told my husband and me that Atlanta was our *land of Milk and Honey,* just like Canaan was the Promised land to the Israelites—but they had to Possess the Land! Glory to God.

Once we possessed the land, God quantum-leaped, expedited, accelerated, and leap-frogged the vision to the front of the LINE!

He needed to see if we had **STAYING POWER!**

CAN WE WEATHER THE STORM or will we fall to the wayside like the rest?

*Yasss Queen, I said it. *

Baby, I know this is a book, but Queen, my Sister, God's beloved Chosen Daughter, you are about to make me PREACH!

I am appointed, anointed, and certified to do it! Thank you, Holy Spirit!

Watch God!

The reason the turns were so sharp…
The reason the snares were so plenty…
The reason the enemy used women who looked like me to set traps against me…

Is Because the ANOINTING over my Life is REAL.

The ASSIGNMENT is REAL.

The FAVOR is REAL.
The CALLING is REAL.
The IMPACT is REAL.

The enemy didn't want the world to have any part of God's goodness and faithfulness to flow through ME!

Oh, but he FAILED. GOD WON, and by default, I WIN TOO! #YasssGod

I am a numbers girl, so let's run the scoreboard, shall we? All the honor, glory, and praise will forever be God's. Between 2019 and 2021, Jesus, Coffee and Prayer has helped more than 140 Women worldwide become international/national best-selling authors, with a vast majority during the pandemic.

Arise Daughters

Under my tutelage or platform by faith, countless women have stepped up to play their royal positions in the home and the marketplace as speakers, authors, or new/emerging business leaders.

Global connections from the USA, Canada, Australia, India, Egypt, New Zealand, Nigeria, Ghana, Jamaica, and everywhere else in between have been formed.

Women are stepping up to the plate and leading with the heart of Christ, Sisterhood, and ridiculous Faith.

My Queens, as I affectionately call them, are also securing the bank. This includes me too!

Not only did God use my vessel to impact, reach, and touch His daughters through my marketplace ministry and business opportunities provided, but He more than tripled my income during the pandemic. My family stood in lack for nothing and continues to be a resource for our church and community.

Nobody but God.

As we refresh others, God is faithful to refresh us.

All the glory belongs to God for all the things He has done!

Queen, Daughter of the Most-High God, I leave you with this.
It is your time to Arise.
It is your time to play your royal position.
It is your time to become unmuzzled.
It is your time to get on your square.

You are the key to unlocking someone else's potential.
You are the breakthrough that someone else is looking for.

You are the vessel that God wants to use to shower His people with love and blessings.

But the God we serve is such a gentleman.

Although He is powerful and your permission is not required, it is requested.

The power of your **YES**- followed by your *FAITH MOVE* in tangible actions will set the captives FREE, starting with YOU!

Arise, Queen.

Set yourself free, and every person God Divinely attached to be set free though your obedience.
I look forward to seeing you at the very top!
Your Sister in Christ,

~Dr. Nakita Davis

Dr. Nikki Zeigler was truly "Born to Lead." As a Prolific Speaker, Branding and Masters Coach, she has been anointed to bring out the inner leader in others. With her background and expertise in Marketing, Branding and Public Relations as well as Advertising, Coach Nikki has set her sights and energy on making a difference by empowering Entrepreneurs, Christian Leaders, Pastors, Ministers, Speakers and Artists to reach for the stars, achieve their goals and fulfill their God-given Destiny.

Dr. Nikki is President of The Herprenuer Network, an organization geared toward Christian women in business. Dr. Nikki is the Executive Publisher of the HBCU Magazine, online Business Professional Magazine for HBCU Attendees and Alumni. Dr. Nikki is the Founder of The Life Christian College, online school that allows Life, Business and Masters Coaches to get their Certification.

YOU MUST REMOVE THE DEAD BODIES!

Dr. Nikki Zeigler

For years I used to carry a lot of dead weight in my life. The weight was so unbearable. I didn't understand what was happening to me in my mind, my spirit, and my heart. I would see myself drifting away during important conversations and I would constantly ask God why I was here. I was so confused, to the point that I wanted to kill myself because I had so much on my mind. I was carrying so many people, so many responsibilities and so much pain that I needed God to remove my whole being. I often had bad dreams of carrying people—not one person but lots of people. During the dream I saw myself carrying five people at one time, and I was strong but as the dreams continued to come, periodically my strength began to leave me. I went to my bishop and asked him to explain the dream to me and the first thing he said to me was, "Why are you carrying dead bodies? Do you know how heavy they are?" When he asked me these questions I began to weep because I felt these dreams were directing me to let some things and people go that I had been holding on to.

I was always the person who people could count on to be there for them. I was always the person who was just a phone call away, but when it was time for me to count on someone no one was anywhere to be found. So I began to examine myself. I went on a major fast and started praying more. As I finished my fast, I knew I had to strip off every weight, in particular all of the dead bodies that had attached themselves to my life and my destiny. God started speaking to me, telling me I had to let the dead bodies go. "Let us also lay aside every weight and that sin that clings so closely and let us run with perseverance the race that is set before us looking to Jesus the pioneer and perfecter of our faith." We must understand that dead weight can destroy our destiny if we allow it.

The one thing we must realize is that weight can cause us to miss out on our purpose. I was living the good life I thought God had for me because I didn't hear God's assignment for my life, so I did what I wanted to do and lived out of God's will for over 15 years. Sometimes as women we can be so emotional, not knowing God has a perfect plan for our lives. We must learn how to trust God in all things and watch him show up in our lives. I made a lot of mistakes in life trying to be God for a lot of people, and that hindered my blessings. I was pursuing things for all the wrong reasons and God wasn't pleased with me at all. It showed me that I had a sabotaging spirit that was attached to my life, and it needed to be broken and removed immediately. I began researching what that meant. I wasn't familiar with the sabotaging spirit.

When I began to research, I found out that this spirit was a part of my family, and I was shocked. I found out that the dead bodies were a part of a generational curse that was attached to my name. I was pursuing things for all the wrong reasons, and I was settling for what came easy and comfortably. In this season God had to shift my mindset. I was settling for anything and anybody just to get attention. I had been pursuing an affair with my ex-husband for three years because I didn't want to let him go and I was comfortable with him. This caused a lot of pain to a lot of people, including my children, so there was a curse on my life because my family was OK with sleeping together outside of marriage. I knew I was wrong for doing what I did but I was so wrapped up in being comfortable with him. He was considered a dead body that was holding me back from the assignment that God had for me, but I was too blind to see the weight that was causing me to lose my mind. I heard God tell me to run away and to leave him alone, but I didn't listen, so God removed everything from me.

I lost my apartment, my car and almost lost my mind. I wanted to give up, but I heard God say, "You must die to yourself and let me lead you." I didn't understand what he meant about the death of myself so once again I began to research these words and, in the Bible, it showed me in his word that God wants us to let him have full control over our thoughts, our minds and our hearts. I had to remove myself from my situation. I had to ask my kids to forgive me for my wrongdoing, and I had to repent daily until the taste of my ex-husband was removed from my mind. Once I decided to allow God to lead me in the path he wanted me to go, that's when my life began to shift.

My desires to do wrong slowly began to leave me. I saw myself reading my Bible more and I got into God's presence. Sometimes we can be so caught up in our sin that we don't realize what we're doing to our lives. That's where the self-sabotaging came into my life. I was carrying a lot of dead bodies, consisting of family members who God had told me to remove out of my life, friends who were only with me for what I had to offer them and people who wanted to pull on my anointing because of what I could do for them.

Every day I had to learn how to show up for God. And I had to start loving the person I saw in the mirror, not people. As I started releasing the dead bodies, I began to be bolder for God. He started giving me a spirit of discernment and showing me who to be there for. With God's help, I had to create a future that lined up with the promises of God. I was too busy pretending to be someone God never wanted me to become so I had to learn to let God lead me in all ways. I was so afraid of rejection that I never let God perform a miracle in my life. But once I let that rejection spirit go, that was when he sent my husband to me, and my life has never been the same. I have never been this happy before in my whole life because I decided to let dead bodies go and let God send me what he wanted me to have, and that was PEACE. I am a living testimony, and I will tell you this day, we must learn how to let God lead us in the way we should go. I am learning every day that I want to be like Jesus, no matter what that looks like. I am so glad that God has forgiven me for the things I did to him and myself.

As a mother and grandmother, Brenda Carroll Lofton has served as the Senior Pastor of House of Refuge International Ministries for 14 years. She is also the Founder, and CEO of Sistaz Can We Talk Women's Ministries, which caters to women of all ages, including teenage girls. Through this ministry, Lofton has ministered and imparted into the lives of women for over two decades.

Lofton is part of a 32-year-old family recording group, which has produced two albums. This avenue of ministry has allowed her to travel all over the world, to include ministering to God's people within the prison systems. She also serves as a liaison between India and the United States through her apostolic missions to help with funding and poverty.

Lofton has received a diploma in Accounting from Blackhawk Technical College and is currently pursuing her bachelor's degree in Psychology at The Grand Canyon University.

I'LL WAIT!!!
Brenda Carroll Lofton

Have you ever said, "I'm waiting for an answer from God?" I believe all have said it. Waiting is trusting and having the patience to see what the answer will be without interfering. Often, we say that we're waiting on God, only to realize that we are not waiting because when you're waiting, you're trusting as well and you're trusting God that everything is and will be all right. We say that a lot, but our actions don't prove it. Waiting on God to answer, you can feel a multitude of emotions like frustration. You feel alone and alienated; one minute you're crying and the next minute you're smiling. One minute everything is all right and the next you're wondering what is going on. You are trying to figure out how to help God fix it.

The scripture says, *But they that wait upon the LORD shall renew their strength; they shall mount up with wings as eagles; they shall run, and not be weary; and they shall walk, and not faint.* Isaiah 40:31, KJV

What does it mean? That as we wait on God our strength is renewed to continue to move forward and wait in a new strength to see what God is doing if we stay still. To give an example of what I'm saying, a few years ago, we were having service in a small room. We had service there for about four years, but the ceiling began to leak, so we moved into a bigger room across the hall. The landlord did not like that we were in that room, but we had nowhere else to go at that time. The room was too small and did not meet the needs of the ministry as it was growing. I prayed and was waiting on an answer from the Lord. I received in the mail an advertisement for a 90 thousand square foot building that was way too big but had potential to do big things in, and maybe we could purchase it. The kitchen was an industrial kitchen with everything in it. It would seat 300 people in the fellowship hall. It had 12 classrooms upstairs and six offices. Downstairs was the fellowship hall and more offices. The building was for rent, and God said it was ours. We were excited so we moved into it. We were there for four years paying rent of $3500 and $4000 in utilities bills for four months of each winter. We did that with about 15 people to carry the ministry. It became difficult to manage this building as it began to fall apart. The foundation was coming apart, the ceiling began to leak, and it was going to take $250,000 to fix the heating in the boiler room. Needless to say, it was time to make some decisions. Here I was waiting on God to answer again.

Waiting on God as you pray takes a lot of patience, and I thought I had a lot. You heard me say I THOUGHT! The word of God says, *in your patience possess ye your souls*. Luke 21:19, KJV. I've had several experiences where I thought with everything in me, I was waiting on God, as I am sure you have as well.

I thought with all my heart, soul and mind that I was waiting on God to move in this situation, only to hear God say to me, "I'm waiting on you." And when He said that to me, I was devastated because three times I verbalized, "I'm just waiting on God." A prophet came to me and said, "God said to tell you He's waiting on you." I heard it and I didn't hear it. And I kept moving forward, still feeling in my heart and in my mind that I was really waiting to hear from God when to move, how to strategically move, so I could make sure that I was totally in his divine will and not his permissive will. That was most important to me, to know for myself that I was surely waiting for the divine will of God for my life. Then the word of the Lord came again and said, "I am waiting on you." Again, I said, "I am waiting on God to tell me what to do and I said I'm waiting on God." I heard it and I didn't hear it.

I began to move forward as if I was still waiting on God! Pretty sad now that I am on the other side of it. It was also very embarrassing, to say the least. It reminded me of a story I once heard about a man that was stranded on an island and he was praying for God to send him help. God sent him a ship, he sent him a raft and a boat, he died and then said, "God I was waiting on you to save me" and God said, "I sent you a ship, a raft and a boat and you sat there still praying and waiting" (unknown author).

For a third time again, a prophet said to me, "God said He's waiting for you." I was devastated. I finally said to God, "What are you waiting for me to do?" and He said, "I'm waiting for you to trust Me!" Boy, that messed my whole life up because I was seriously, wholeheartedly waiting for God and all the time he was waiting for me to trust what I heard and move in what I heard him say. It broke my little heart, but as soon as I was sure I heard Him, I moved. The whole problem was that it took me so long when I should have heard it the first time. I wasted a lot of time and I'm sure I missed some things by not hearing the first time he spoke. Big lesson learned. I also learned, sometimes when you think you're waiting on God, He is waiting for you! What I'm saying to you is to open up your spiritual ears and open up your heart. Keep your heart and your ear to the breast of God and hear him when he speaks the first time.

You must have endurance and patience when you're waiting. Luke 21:19, KJV says, *In your patience processes ye your soul,* and I realized for the first time in my later years in life that I needed more patience; that's what caused me to make a lot of mistakes in my life. I didn't have patience to wait on the right things. When you have a microwave mentality and you want everything in a hurry, you make a lot of decisions that you don't realize are wrong. You don't know what the problem is until after you have made the decision. What it adds up to is your patience is very thin and it will hurt you more than help you in the future.

For a second just stop and think how you wait or don't wait for things to happen in your everyday life. I'LL WAIT. Are you a person who says I need to do 15 things in one hour? You don't plan and prioritize things, so you are not rushing your day? Pay attention all around you and in every area of your life—everything that you do, do you want to hurry up? The scripture says, *Don't be anxious for anything and with all prayer and supplication make your petitions known to Him.* So when you pray and make your petitions known to him, he never promised that once He heard them that in the next five minutes or the next 15 minutes or the next day or the next two days that it was going to be answered. He said that he would answer but he didn't say when, so that is where our patience will come in. Think about it—how much patience do you have? I'LL WAIT.

God has taken me on a journey in this season in my life. It seemed to me that it was kind of a late time in life to learn this lesson, but

I promise you, it is never too late for God to teach you anything that you need to help you navigate in this life. You will always be learning lessons as long as you live. Just recently God spoke to me and told me it was time for me to move on. He told me in a dream, "I called you to the nations and you are not ready." When I woke up, He directed me to Jeremiah chapter 1. Oh My GOODNESS! I was like, "God, are you kidding me?" I was scared and thought, *How could I have failed doing what God meant for me to do all this time?* The voice was so loud and profound there was no mistake that it was the voice of God. I felt like, *How much time have I wasted?*

I have been doing ministry since 1986, when I heard Him say in a seven-day shut-in (yes, we had shut-ins in those days) that He had called me to walk in the vocation of an evangelist. Here I was an ordained evangelist, then a pastor, then in 2014 affirmed as an apostle. I felt like Abraham. I was single, no kids at home, had open heart surgery in 2011, eight heart attacks and one stroke later, starting a new journey. I was so afraid. I had no other instructions from God except to go. I spoke with an apostle to try to get some clarity. He said to me my journey was a lot like his; he started late as well. Now mind, you we are in a pandemic, where was I going? This is preparation time. I spoke to my mentor, and she confirmed that I had heard correctly. My lease was up at my apartment, and it appeared things were all lined up according to what God said. I put all my things in storage and moved. I was waiting on God! This time was different, though, because I had no doubt that I heard GOD, but where was I going?

This was really the Abraham experience. I am sure my family and friends were saying, "What is she doing?" God just keeps showing up in unusual ways to reassure me I heard Him correctly. He even showed me in another dream that I was headed in the right direction but in my eyes, it still didn't look like it. I was still waiting, sometimes frustrated, lots of crying, but still waiting.

I was grateful for the door that was opened for me to have a roof over my head without any explanation, just grace and understanding that I was following the will of God. It was hard because I felt like I was homeless, and for what? I was always able to take care of myself, pay my bills, do whatever was necessary to make sure I was secure. Well, here I was; I didn't know my next step or my next move and was feeling very sad and completely out of control of what was going on in my life. One night I was crying my eyes out and praying, asking God, "WHAT IS REALLY GOING ON?" I told my sister, "It's ok, I know how to fix it; I know how to take care of myself. I'm going to get my apartment back and that's it!" I laid down and went to sleep and at 7AM my phone rang. The woman of God on the other end of the phone said to me, "God said you need to just WAIT! I've got you! Yes, you heard me, you're on the right track; just be still and WAIT!" I was just floored! God heard me and answered me quickly so I would not make a mess. Then I had to repent to God for getting out of His will in my thoughts. This was a tough season and I had never been in a place like this before. Crying, I said, "Ok I'LL WAIT!" A few more days went by, and I was back there again. You know how that goes: We say ok to God, but the enemy heard it too and came immediately and stole that reassurance that I had to wait. There I was crying and praying again. All of a sudden, I heard a message come up on my Facebook messenger. The name that came up I didn't recognize, and I said, "Who is that?" I opened the message and it was a video. The guy in the video says, "Hey you! Yes you, God told me to send this message to you. He says you need to wait. You need to be still because if you wait, there is a great reward for you. I will give you double for your trouble. I promise your waiting will not be in vain." He said, "Waiting on God isn't always easy, but it seems like it is taking forever." Of course, you know by now my mouth was hanging open. I was looking around the room to see if there are some holes in the walls and somebody heard me and decided to play a trick on me. I was like, *Is this really real? Does this stuff really happen?* God just supernaturally sent me this video because he saw I was about to lose it!

Yes, God is concerned about you. He is concerned about what you are going through. Weeping may endure for a night but Joy—yes, I said it—Joy will come in the morning. You are probably asking when is the morning? I say, when you wake up! When you realize that your joy will come from God. When you see that you can't do it anyway and you're waiting patiently on Him. So the guy says to me, "I want you to rejoice when I give you this word." Listen, sometimes we are waiting to be healed, we are waiting for a mate, we are waiting for a good job, we are waiting, waiting, waiting and realistically, we say, "I'm tired of waiting" and then we begin to say, "WHEN? IM TIRED OF WAITING." Just hold on because if you wait to see what God is doing in this waiting season, it will be worth the wait.

The scripture in Psalm 27:14 says, *Wait on the Lord and be of good courage and he shall strengthen thine heart; wait, I say, on the Lord.*

As a leader others' expectations of you are that you should be perfect. We are not allowed to go through anything, so we try to prove to others that we are always on top of the world. Well, that is what is killing us. Stop trying to feel something other than what you really feel. I was feeling some kind of way about not having a place to call my own, not knowing where I was going or what I was doing, just the word wait. It has truly been an Abraham experience. That's all I could say when people would ask me. "What are you doing?" and I would just say, "I'm just waiting."

God promised if you wait you will be healed, your ministry will flourish, your life will never be the same, your relationships will never be the same. Your finances will never be the same, you will have a better understanding, you will have better spiritual vision. Your life will never be the same if you could just wait!

He will give you double for your trouble! The scripture says, in Isaiah 61:7, MSG,

Because you got a double dose of trouble and more than your share of contempt, your inheritance in the land will be doubled and your joy go on forever.

When the waiting season has passed, your reward is just as great! You must wait—I said you must wait! There are some things you will have to endure to get through this season, but it is worth it. Stand still and stand firm on what God says for you. Don't move, be still!

This is how you wait:

1. Submit yourself to God and resist the devil.
2. Fast and pray.
3. Consecrate yourself.
4. Read the Bible daily.
5. Talk to someone who can help you sort out your feelings.
6. Listen carefully to the voice of God.
7. Yield completely to Him.

As I am writing this chapter, I believe I'm almost at the end of this waiting season. I've been in it about six months now and I can see the light at the end of the tunnel. It has been a tough time but very rewarding. Many times, I wanted to give up but God stayed right there with me, sometimes supernaturally but His presence was always around me, through things like the video that I spoke of earlier, through the voice of a great woman of God who continually prayed and kept me lifted up, through others who had no idea what they did or said that kept me focused. I lost some people along the way, but I gained another place in God for the next level. I received the gift of patience from the Lord. I learned to be quiet when I wanted to scream. I made a few mistakes along the way, I missed God along the way, but it's ok. So I say to you, if God said it, do it!

YOU MUST WAIT! Don't get in a hurry for the season to be over, JUST WAIT! Don't create your own way to stop the pain of waiting, JUST WAIT! God is faithful to us. He loves us and He wants the best for us all. He knows what we need and what is best for us. You must choose to wait! Yield yourself in your mind and in your heart to say to God, I'LL WAIT!

As a native of Philadelphia, Jalima Cook was raised by her mother who instilled the importance of pressing toward greatness in all things. Throughout her life, she taught her a "no excuse" philosophy - a principle she applies in every area of her life, even today.

With plans to attend law school after graduating high school, God redirected Cook to seminary school. Years later, she earned her Master's Degree in Divinity. With 20 years of experience serving in various ministry and leadership roles, Cook teaches the gospel, with a passion for teaching on vision and purpose.

Cook (wife, mother, preach, writer, visionary leader, and entrepreneur), currently resides in Kansas City, Missouri with her husband of 14 years, their four children, and fur baby.

FINDING GOD IN DARKNESS

Jalima Cook

Have you ever heard the saying "There is always at least one person going through the same as you?" Even though that may be a true statement, I used to despise it because I just knew that I was the only person experiencing the mental turmoil that I secretly struggled with daily. It would be years of battling with my mental health before I would realize that I did not have to suffer in silence, that there were others, in fact, going through the same as me. After living through a very dark time in my life, I decided to share my story with hope that it will trigger those who read it to know that God has not left them. Finding God in such times may seem impossible, but it is in these times that God is in fact closer than ever.

Here is my story of my personal battle with mental illness that at one point had me stuck and in the dark. Depression, anxiety, and suicidal ideation plagued my life for a long time and played a major behind-the-scenes role in my daily existence. I have shared bits and pieces over the years, but have always held back some due to fear, embarrassment, and being overly concerned about people's opinions. These things combined were the perfect recipe for me to build a facade. Because what does a facade offer? Safety! However, the safety I thought I was successfully building was actually keeping me bound.

Allow me to share with you how each of these struggles have played a role in my life:

Suicidal Ideation.

A word over the years that haunted me and tortured my mind with ideas of relief rooted in untruth. At different points in my life, I believed it was the best way to deal with the seemingly unbearable troubles and problems in my life.

Depression.

This word has defined my state of being more times than I used to care to admit out of fear of rejection or being deemed unfit. It kept me in bed some days, totally uninterested in participating in life, and other days had me only wanting to eat brownie sundaes in my pjs, in the dark, while binging on reality TV. It also had its extremely "high" days when I would move 100 miles per minute to get a million things done at the speed of light.

At least that is what it felt like in *my* mind. The highs and lows of depression are truly torturous!

Anxiety.

My regular routine in life that jeopardized my inner peace and led me down the path that always consisted of worry, distrust, and confusion. It made it hard to focus, difficult to breathe, and was often the root of crying spells that sent me in a cycle of "Jalima, you suck" recitations that convinced my mind into believing everything opposite of who God said I was.

Here is a shocking truth: I still battle with anxiety some days! I used to deny this, but God, counseling, and my medical doctor helped me see why this denial was an unhealthy practice rooted in pride and fear.

So this is me and because of suicide, depression, and anxiety, I have had to learn to fight daily to win the battle with my mind. These are the battles I have fought and have learned that they do not define me because, as a child of God, I know that my very existence is rooted in God. However, I did not always believe this truth. It was not until my own attempt at suicide that I realized all the lies I was believing. For years I believed that because I struggled with these things, God could not help me—almost as if my struggle placed me on the outside of God's love and grace. This lie almost ended my life; however, with God, I have fought hard to overcome, win, and be the woman God called me to be.

My journey of finding God in the dark times of my life was birthed when I was not only lost as to what to do with my life, but also when I totally lost sight of how God sees me. I remember the day: I sat on my kitchen floor, shaking, crying, and barely able to breathe. I was having what I later learned was a panic attack and I was dealing with some serious postpartum depression. None of my thoughts were toward hurting my newborn baby, but many of my thoughts were geared toward wanting to escape. It's hard to put into words all the emotions I was feeling because to be honest, they did not make sense. To make things even more complicated I remembered confiding in someone about my unstable emotions and wanting to escape and I was immediately reprimanded. The words spoken to me echoed in me for quite a while: "How could you be so selfish? Why would you do that to your family? You have to be stronger than this!"

Though I understood the intent behind the intended-to-be motivational words, they instead triggered a pain deep within that made me want to escape even more. I was devastated and hurt beyond words. I wanted help, but I was fully convinced that God was mad at me for even feeling this way. Though suicide left my thoughts that day, something else arose within me – disappointment. I sat on that floor asking God over and over again, "Why is this so hard?"

That was not my last bout with suicidal ideations and severe depression. However, it was the beginning of learning how to hide it. I learned how to suppress it. I learned to ignore it. I learned to busy myself just enough so I could be too tired to actually deal with it. I didn't talk to God about it because I was too ashamed. I would try to talk to friends but would often quickly put up my "I'm stronger than this" wall. I call it a wall because I was trapping myself into a way of living that was severely unhealthy and let's be real, FAKE! I was not being true to myself. My family. God. No one! I learned to over-function in every area of life.

I would hide my panic attacks.
I hid my meltdowns.

I sought to be perceived through a perfect lens so I would not have to add people's disappointment to my list of problems.

It took years before it would catch up to me.

Five pregnancies, one of which was a devastating miscarriage, before I would have to face the truth.
A very troubled marriage before I would have to get real.

I graduated with my master's degree while I struggled.
I preached my first sermon while I struggled.
I served as a minister and associate pastor while I struggled.
I was a mommy of four very busy kiddos while I struggled, one of whom was diagnosed with Autism in the midst of it all.
I was drowning, but I would not allow anyone to see I was fighting to keep my head above the water while the weight of life was only pulling me down deeper into a severe depression.

What was I to do?

I *thought* I knew the answer on the night of June 10, 2017—a night that changed my life. It was this night that I found myself with 57 pills in hand, speeding down the interstate, with repetitive racing thoughts screaming louder than ever before, "Jalima, just give up!" I rehearsed how disappointed God must be in me. I recalled shame and re-lived stories of my inadequacy. The overwhelming feeling of rejection clouded my perception and made it difficult for me to realize that I was actually rehearsing lies that led to me and my thoughts fully spiraling out of control. I found the strength to scream out loud, "God, help me! Please!" and those four simple, one-syllable words led to me noticing blue signs on the highway with a white letter "H" in the middle. I followed these signs, which ultimately led to me arriving at a nearby hospital. I sat in the emergency room parking lot and negotiated with my mind: Go in and ask for help or take the pills. Those were really the only two options I thought I had at the moment.

I looked at my phone but could not bring myself to call anyone. I recalled and repeatedly rehearsed the shame speech from years ago. I wanted help. So I screamed out of frustration and pounded on the car steering wheel.

Question after question ran through my mind:
What will my church say?
What will my husband and family say?
What would God say? That was it! I needed to know what God says! Would God want me to get help or give up? The answer was suddenly obvious to me.

Let's pause for a moment.

How many times could the question, "What would God say?" help us in those dark moments in life? You don't have to quote the longest scripture. All it takes is acknowledging this truth: God promises that he will never leave you! There are numerous scriptures in both the Old and New Testament that say this, but my favorite is Deuteronomy 31:8, *"The Lord is the one who will go before you. He will be with you; he will not leave you or abandon you. Do not be afraid or discouraged."* Imagine grabbing hold of this truth and rehearsing these words when you are ready to quit. God's love and compassion for us goes incredibly deep - nothing can take that away. Not even guilt or shame!

I put the pills in the pocket of my hoodie, opened the car door, and with tears pouring down my face, I got out of the car to enter the hospital. Halfway to the door I fell to the ground crying. Chills ran through my body, my chest got heavy, and it literally felt like the pain from years had just knocked me down. The battle to get from the parking lot to the emergency room felt like something was fighting me from entering the building. But I knew that even if I had to crawl, I needed to get in there. Once I was finally inside, I was able to say two words to the nurse: "Help me," and the tears just poured. I dropped all the pills from my pocket onto the counter and the nurse immediately took me back to a hospital room.

They took everything from me – clothes, shoes, rings, and my watch. I sat in the cold room and for the first time in a while I felt safe! I couldn't hurt myself now! I now cried tears of relief. The next few hours were filled with a lot of doctors, nurses, and the inevitable decision to admit me on a three-day psychiatric hold at a local hospital. The doctor said to me, "Jalima, this was too close a call to risk sending you home." I immediately told the doctor a ton of reasons I could not go to a psychiatric hospital.

What would people think?
I had clients!
My children needed me!
My husband had to work!
What would I tell my friends?
And what would my church think? They would disapprove and probably not want me there anymore.

The doctor got very quiet and then looked at me and firmly said, "It's time to get you the help you need. I am not concerned about anything but that. You care about everyone more than yourself. That is not how God wants you to live."

Ouch, she was right! She was so right that I was speechless and no more rebuttals came out of my mouth, as I seriously felt like my lips had been zipped.

The next morning, I was transported to a facility where I'd be spending the next few days and would face some hard truths. Upon arrival, I walked into a cool and dark room and I lay on the very flat bed and just cried and asked myself, "How did I get to this point?" Little did I know, I was about to have an encounter with God that would answer that very question.

As the days progressed it did not take long for me to realize that I was not alone in my battle with my mental health. The 12 women in my unit were all dealing with significant trauma. Many of them had been there a few times and others were convinced that the world would be better without them. I listened to the stories and my internal response was grief. I could feel every story they shared. They all shared stories about feeling alone and just stuck in darkness. Some had tried cutting themselves, taking pills, and others had attempts and were disappointed that they lived through it. Each night I stayed awake all night talking to God (literally) and reading the Bible that I found in the lounge area. I was always awake after everyone else was asleep so the nurses allowed me to sit in the lounge area and read my Bible. They even allowed me access to a pen and notepad so I could write. For hours I would pore over the Word and would write down everything God said. There was so much I was holding onto. I finally had to acknowledge that I had been dealing with depression for way too long and it was time to do something. Time to go on a journey to identify who God says I am so that I could properly replace and redefine the incorrect truths that had taken up residence in my mind. The feat seemed impossible, but the previous 24 hours shook me to the core and I finally could see beyond my circumstances enough to know that God was with me. God was taking what I deemed impossible and showing me the steps necessary to experience healing. I wanted to be delivered from the dark pit of depression.

But how?
Was I too messed up?
Would God really show up in the midst of all of this?
Of course he would! God was with me through it all!

I didn't have to have it all together before I could be rescued! What kind of sense would that make? A lifeguard doesn't wait to rescue a drowning victim! They jump in as soon as there is a sign of distress! In my weakness God sent in reinforcements. I am 100% certain that God aligned every doctor, nurse, and therapist that I came in contact with. I also strongly believe that had I not gone to that hospital, the wake-up call I needed to live would have continued to be delayed. Had I kept hiding, denying, avoiding, and pretending, I would have kept giving in to the lies being fed to me. I had to find God to ultimately be directed by him on finding myself! Finding the Me, He created me to be and not who I thought I had to be!

It was time for surgery and some mental retraining.

My training started with these words: MY GRACE IS SUFFICIENT. These words were stuck in my head. I just kept saying it over and over again to myself until it dawned on me that I needed to pay attention. I don't know about you, but when these types of things happen to me, that is usually my signal that I need to stop what I am doing, attune my ears, and pray. The full scripture comes from 2 Corinthians 12:9, NIV:

> But he said to me, "My grace is sufficient for you, for my power is made perfect in weakness." Therefore, I will boast all the more gladly of my weaknesses, so that Christ's power may rest on me.

This familiar passage jumped off the page differently when I read it this time. All this time I deemed myself unfit and unworthy, but God, my father, was telling me that was not the case because his grace is inexhaustible and it had nothing to do with me earning it or even deserving it. This challenged me because some legalistic teaching in my upbringing only applied grace in certain situations and mental illness was not one of them. Now, as an adult, finally learning that God wanted to help me through my struggle blew my mind! Knowing that I did not have to continue to pretend to be strong because God wanted to be that for me. God wanted to take it. And not only did he take it, he applied his love, grace, and healing power to my struggle and it saved my life!

It is my prayer that more people who may struggle with their mental health will grab hold of the truth that God is always there. Unfortunately, we live in a world where bad things will happen, but God promises to be with us through it. Giving up does not have to be an option. One of the biggest lies I believed was that God could not use me because I struggled with depression and anxiety - THAT ALSO IS NOT TRUE! God does not punish us for our struggle. God offers grace, love, support, and guidance to the best way for life. Darkness cannot win when God is present. Know who God says you are. My favorite reminder is in Ephesians 2:10,

NLT "For we are God's masterpiece. He has created us anew in Christ Jesus, so we can do the good things he planned for us long ago."

God is not finished with you. Every masterpiece has imperfections, but it is those imperfections that define the creator's invaluable purpose for his work of art. Walk in that greatness God created you to be.

As a native of the south suburbs of Chicago, Pamela Kennedy was raised in the foster care system which allowed her to live with several different family members. By the age of 18, she became a statistic as a high school dropout and teen mother.

Defying all odds, Kennedy is a single mother of an amazing young lady who has obtained a college degree and is the founder of a youth organization to help others who are experiencing the challenges of being in the foster care system.

Giving back, Kennedy currently works within the child welfare system, with a passion to become a teacher. Eager to return to the classroom setting, she is currently pursuing her Master's Degree in Sociology with an emphasis on Education.

HELPING UNTIL IT HURTS
LEARNING TO CARRY MY OWN LOAD

Pamela Kennedy

As you embark in reading this chapter let me start off by giving a disclaimer: I am not, nor do I claim to be, an expert in any field. I am simply sharing with you my experiences and my viewpoints regarding them. Now with that being said, let's get started.

If you were to survey a group of the people who are closest to me, many of them would tell you that I am a very giving and motivating person. I am a helper by nature; in fact, it is almost instinctive for me to try to help if I see someone, especially those I hold dear, in need of anything. I have always taken the stance that I help because I would want it if I were in need of assistance, plus it follows one of the golden rules concerning treating others how you want to be treated. In fact, Proverbs 3:27 encourages us not to withhold good from others if it is within our power to do good. Many people see nothing wrong with that, especially those who are receiving the help, but I have learned that sometimes we as people can find ourselves "helping until it hurts."

I don't know about you, but the pandemic gave me an entirely new way of looking at life. Before the pandemic, I feel that I was merely going through the motions. I was so involved with taking care of others, working, going to school and participating in church that I was not taking the time to live and enjoy the life that God had blessed me with.

In fact, I found myself feeling burnt out, overworked, stressed and overall unproductive. I felt that I was merely in survival mode all the time. If I was not at work, I was dealing with family, running errands for children, trying to finish school assignments at the very last minute and in the attempt the practice of self-care I would be up until 1 or 2 a.m. just to enjoy a moment of silence while everyone else was sleeping. I did this for years only to realize that I was getting nowhere. One day I looked up and everyone around me that I had been helping and or caring for was enjoying their life and living out their dreams and I was sitting there merely existing and feeling stressed out and overwhelmed. I can remember having the conversation with God while sitting in my car outside my job; it went something like this: "Lord, you told me that you would never put on me more than I can bear. This load that I'm carrying is pretty heavy... are you sure that you have the right person?" It was then that God gave me the vision of me pulling a pretty red wagon. This wagon was not just full, it was overflowing with all types of things. I could clearly see myself struggling to pull it and things were falling off and I was trying to gather them while still trying to pull the load.

My first response to this vision was deciding that I had way too much on my plate and I needed to take a break. So I contacted my pastor and informed her that with everything that I had going on, I would need to be relieved of my responsibilities for teaching youth Bible Study. Because, of course, I couldn't just not take care of my family, and school and work were not options for me to quit. So I attempted to quit the one thing that I was consistently doing for the Lord. For me the choice seemed very easy. This would allow me an entire evening to try relaxing and complete tasks that I couldn't normally complete because I would be at church. Anyone who has had an active role as a leader in ministry knows that my pastor was totally against this idea. She informed me that she did not believe that God wanted me to do this; however, she stated that if I needed a break she understood. For the next several weeks I did not teach. The interesting thing, however, is that I did not complete any additional tasks and even worse, I did not get any opportunities to relax either. In fact, people got wind that I was not attending church on Thursday night and begin to schedule other things for me. God has one heck of a sense of humor.

Finding myself even more stressed and overwhelmed, I did what I should have done in the first place and I had a talk with my creator. The conversation went something like this:

Lord, what am I doing wrong?

Silence...

Lord, are you there? Do you even care?

Still silence...

Now frustrated... *Lord, what do you want me to do?*

Finally in a clear voice I heard, **You already know...** and the red wagon appeared again, this time with even more crap in it.

I know, Lord, this is a heavy load you have given me.

Now, now, I didn't give you all of that. You need to take inventory.

For several nights after that I just couldn't sleep. I kept seeing this wagon, but I struggled to see what I was doing that God had not assigned me to do. In regular God fashion, just in the nick of time, I returned to school and was given a very interesting assignment. The very first assignment was to take inventory of everything that I did for three consecutive days. To be honest with you, I felt like it was a waste of time and that I could be doing something more productive; however, because it was for a grade, I humored my professor and completed the assignment. For the next three days I itemized what I did each hour. This included my morning routine, daily activities, as well as the number of hours that I slept. On the fourth day when I had to review the results, it was a very eye-opening experience for me. The very first thing I noticed was the number of hours that I was asleep. At that time, I was averaging three to four hours a night of rest. The next thing that I noticed was the number of times throughout the day I was off task because I was doing something for someone else. The final thing that I noticed that was very disturbing to me was that throughout my day I was so busy taking care of everything for everyone else that I was not taking the time to spend with God or even care enough about myself to eat. On two out of the three days I did not have my first meal of the day until nearly 3 p.m., and I was lucky to get a daily scripture in. This explained so many things. Almost every day before this assignment I felt sluggish, battled headaches throughout the day, and always felt like I was trying to catch up on my work and sleep. So what did I do, you may ask.

First and foremost, I prayed about it and I asked God to help me to prioritize. Matthew 6:33 tells us to seek ye first the kingdom of God. This resulted in me going on somewhat of a hiatus for a while. During that time, I only did what was absolutely necessary. Things such as prayer, going to work, completing my schoolwork, and family time were the only things I did. This eliminated a great deal of stress and allowed me to get a great deal of rest. Next, I began to go back to church; however, I went so that I could be fed. Too many times people like me who find themselves helping until it hurts are people who pour into others and find themselves running on empty because no one is pouring into them. This was not an easy task for me. There were many questions as to why I was not being as active in church as I once was—whispers about how I must have sinned against God and felt convicted. But worst of all, my children that I taught and worked with for several years repeatedly asked me to come back to teach. Pricked in the heart by this, soon I was back at it again, doing as much as I could for as many people as possible. I found myself back in the cycle all over again.

After a while I found myself not wanting to get out of bed, and if I made it to work, when I got home from work, I was so full of stress and anxiety that I would sit outside in my car trying to overcome the overwhelming anxiety that I felt. The idea of even having to interact with the people I loved most began to cause panic attacks. The sad thing is that it was nothing that my family had done to cause these emotions. After dealing with this and suffering in silence, one day while sitting on my couch, I went to rub my eye and realized that the right side of my face was numb. I immediately began to panic. I felt that I might be having a stroke. I was 37 years old and other than some blood pressure issues; I was overall a healthy person. I told my sister who was with me what I was feeling and she urged me to go to the hospital.

When I arrived my blood pressure was extremely high and they rushed me to the emergency room. During this time, I began to pray, as many of us do, saying, "Lord, if you let me overcome this, I promise I will do things differently." The doctors checked me out and concluded that I had not had a stroke; however, they wanted me to follow up with my primary physician as soon as possible. I followed up with her as suggested and she began to ask me what I felt was causing the fluctuation in my blood pressure. I began to discuss my daily routines. She acknowledged that I was quite busy but she knew there was something that I was not telling her. After some probing, I shared with her the anxiety and panic attacks that I had been experiencing and she suggested that I try a medication to assist in calming my nerves. Because I am not one to take medication, I asked if there were any other alternatives and she suggested that I try counseling. At first, I was a little hesitant however the recent scare of a stroke helped to remove any hesitation that I had.

During my first session my therapist asked me the infamous question... why are you here? I jokingly said because my doctor made me. She humored me for a while but began to ask why I felt so stressed. As I began to share with her what I felt was causing the anxiety and panic attacks she kept asking a simple question: Well, why? The more she asked that the more I began to ask the same question. Finally, I asked myself, *Why do I do what I do when I really don't want to?* It took me awhile but when I was finally honest with myself, I realized that I was helping people even if it hurt me because I was afraid of losing or disappointing them in some way. As I began to dig deeper into this, I realized that it had a lot to do with the trauma of my childhood, most of which I did not take the time to properly deal with. As someone who was raised in foster care, I was often made to feel as though my best was not good enough, and if I didn't live up to others' expectations, I would have to be moved to another home, which happened more than once. These experiences were things that I carried with me in my wagon that were given to me by people other than God. The wagon experience for me was very life changing. It allowed me to see that I was carrying around things that I inherited naturally through genetics, things that were cast on to me through interactions and experiences, and things that I picked up along the way willingly. All of these things were overshadowing what God had given me. Once I took the time to clean out my wagon and began to truly take inventory, I was able to deal with the unnecessary baggage. This involved me giving a lot of things over to Jesus, as suggested in Psalm 55:22. Now I carry a much lighter load in life. Don't get me wrong; it's definitely not always easy and every so often, I have to take inventory again to make sure that I haven't picked up anything that's not supposed to be there, but with God's help I have been able to carry my load.

Believe it or not, for those of us who are helpers by nature, *no* is not an easy thing for us to say. It has been one of the hardest yet best things I have ever done for myself. After taking inventory and prioritizing things in my life, I found myself beginning to slip back into old habits. When people would ask me to do things that were conflicting with my schedule and or priorities, I noticed that it was hard for me to say no. Instead, I would begin to try to strategize and reorganize my schedule to try to accommodate the request even if it meant inconveniencing myself. I began to feel distress and anxiety resurface, so I knew it was time for me to check my wagon again. This time it was easier for me to see what didn't belong in my wagon and I quickly began correcting my behavior.

I believe the struggle that I had most was battling with the idea that I was able to assist. In my mind I am always able to assist, but in his usual fashion God met me in yet another unexpected place. On a drive to work one morning while listening to a radio station they were discussing the importance of letting God be God. As I listened the speaker was talking about how we as humans interfere and put our hands in things that God is working on. Right there in my car it hit me—there were so many times in my life where I thought that I was helping but I was interfering with valuable lessons that God was attempting to teach those that I was assisting. I have learned that there is a difference between helping and enabling. In too many instances in my life I feel that I may have enabled people by actually helping them because it took them longer to learn the lesson that God was trying to teach them. We have to make sure that we are not playing God by providing a way of escape for people. This is not to say that you can't help anyone; we just have to stay prayerful and make sure that what we call help is not actually enabling someone.

Life after the revelation that I received has been a lot less stressful. I still help others; however, I do not do it at the cost of my sanity or health. I have learned that it's okay to say *no*. During this process many people have distanced themselves from me and the loss of a few of those relationships really hurt. However, through the hurt I was able to learn and see the difference between those who loved me unconditionally versus those who loved me on condition of what I could do for them. Since I have begun to take inventory, prioritize, learn to say no and move out of God's way, I have had time to complete the tasks that God has given me—things such as start a non-profit, work on my master's degree, repair my credit, purchase a house, and improve my health. They have all been on my personal to do list for several years; however, I was too busy helping others to achieve those goals. I am proud to say I have not only completed that to-do list, but I also started another and just by taking the time to complete this chapter I have checked yet another box on that list. If you get nothing else from this chapter, I pray that you learn that you are important enough for you to care about yourself if no one else does. The load that you are carrying consists of what God has given you, what others have passed to you, and what you have picked up along the way. Any time you feel that your load is too much for you to carry, take time to take inventory and prioritize your load, because you may be helping until it hurts while hindering you or someone else.

Dyrell Denise Lee is the founder of Hazel Denise House, Inc. - a future transitional home for those coming out of the foster care system. Under the umbrella of this organization, she has another company named Princess To Queens; a mentor program for girls, ages 14 to 19 years old.

Lee is also the founder and owner of Beautiful and Handsome One Events, and Life Celebration Events, LLC, located in Chicago, IL. Her passion is the "Orphan of America" (also known as foster children), and she is ready to take the stand for the fatherless and motherless. She is also the author of Let Me Introduce My X's, which also has an accompanying workbook.

Residing in Naperville, IL with two adult children, Lee was ready to begin this journey; while understanding that now is the time to come out of hiding and let her voice be heard across the world.

TRAUMA IN THE WOMB
Dyrell Lee

Traumatized people persistently feel unsafe inside their souls: The past is alive in the form of a nibble, eating away at the interior discomfort of their heart and mind.

Hello Dyrell! Why are you sitting in the corner? You are walking in greatness now, your life came together according to God's will and his ordained purpose for your life. Yes, I know you were abused sexually, physically, verbally, mentally, and emotionally. On top of that you experienced trauma in the womb, then your mother died five years later. Yes, you ended up in foster care until the age of 21 years, felt like an outcast by family members. I want to say to you, come out of the corner, "GET UP, STAND TALL, WALK IN YOUR DOMINION, YOUR AUTHORITY, YOUR POWER. YOU ARE BEAUTIFUL INSIDE AND OUT! Your past is what it is—YOUR PAST. God has your future in place. You never thought you would make it over 18 because of the five suicide attempts. Beautiful Butterfly, you are living now and snatching others out of the hands of Satan. Well, you are over 50 and I have great news, younger me; let me tell you how you got freed from trauma, now walking in your freedom.

This is how it started. "Lord, why? Why? Why?" I'm 40 years of age, why so much pain, disappointment, and abuse? I'm tired of being tired of life; not being happy with the hand I was given. I didn't ask to be here. At the age of 46 I was deep into homelessness for seven years; no one knew the extent of it. I wore a mask. I never stopped doing ministry and serving others and feeding the homeless when I was homeless myself. I was living here and there, sleeping in my car. I was out of character, doing things to survive in these streets. What the hell is going on? I better not go to hell trying to do right. Life just don't like me. Help me, Lord!! Please Help me.

In 2017 the Lord started talking to me during my suffering. I was going through domestic violence; Lord, this is not the time to study new revelations; don't you see my suffering? Do you care? What did I do? I heard the word "orphan" repeatedly for days. I decided to study it. Well, I studied the word in depth and guess what I found out? I'm an orphan, me at this age. I thought orphans lived in other countries, not in America. I found out I'm an orphan in the natural; you can have an orphan spirit as well. I'm focused on the orphan in the natural. An orphan is a child whose parents died when their child was too young to care for themselves. I was orphaned at five. WOW! That was news to me. But how does all that connect with my life journey? Everything is about to make sense as you keep reading my story.

Let's talk about this trauma in the womb. My mother at the age of 15 had a devastating experience with three young men that she knew at a party. She was violated sexually and nine months later, in early August, I was born. Can you imagine how she was treated during her pregnancy during the 60s and not married? She experienced rejection, was abandoned by some family members and she was on her own, unstable. I'm in the womb experiencing everything that she is experiencing. Now the baby is born, already in spiritual warfare.

My mother was unstable in her living arrangements, always moving. I was told that she loved her children and she read the word of God to us all the time. She kept a job. She knew she was on her own. Without the help of her family, she had to do what she needed to do. What I knew of my mother was that she loved people and she took care of those who were in need (she fed those who were hungry). Her home was open to the broken.

In February 1975, these men took my mom out of the apartment on an ambulance gurney, so I ran in the corner of my bedroom balled up with my head between my legs, looking at the vinyl floor with clowns (to this day I don't like clowns), crying. That was the last day I would see my mother; at 21 years of age, she expired here on the earth. Her time here had ended. What was about to take place in the next 45 years would shift my life from sadness, pain, disappointment, bitterness, and anger, to sweet.

When my mother died, I thought this was the beginning of my trauma. I was a very quiet and shy little girl, very defensive and would fight if you pressed the right button. I was afraid of people, especially adults. I had identity, abandonment, and low self-esteem issues and also received all forms of abuse: physical, mental, sexual, neglect and domestic. Domestic violence doesn't just happen in marriage. All of this abuse took place within the place that was to protect me, which was family. I was so afraid of adults because of the physical and mental trauma from certain family members.

What led up to me going to foster care? Here we go. I was sent to live with relatives. I was so unstable throughout my childhood and adult life. My sister and brother were always stable in their living arrangements; they were always together, and to this day they are very close to each other. My siblings didn't know me in the way they needed to know me as their oldest sibling. They are more stable than I. Earlier I stated that my mother was unstable while I was in her womb; can you see how my trauma is starting to connect? Keep reading; it will make sense at the end of my brief story.

The trauma continued. The first sexual abuse happened months after the passing of my mother, in the summer, by a stranger in the gangway next to my great-grandmother's apartment building. The second sexual abuse was with a family member for years. It started at the age of eight and there were men involved until I finally ended up in foster care. I still have physical scars from the abuse that took place when I was a child. I ended up with Children and Family Services (foster care) due to the fact that I was five minutes late from curfew and didn't want another black eye, which I had gotten many times from a relative. I was told to tell everyone that I was playing and fell and hit my eye. The verbal abuse was outrageous but what could I do? I was a defenseless child without rights.

I was under the guardianship of the state of Illinois until I turned 21 years of age. I was blessed that they kept me that long. The director told me I had potential to be a leader one day and my acting out and anger issues were just for a moment. Most of the young ladies that turned 18 were let go into the world without a plan or anywhere to go. During my time with DCFS I was in and out of five foster and three group homes. In one of the group homes I stayed in for three years, there were 25 different personalities, ages, race, and backgrounds. I liked that home. I felt safety there. We fought a lot but there were no abusive adults.

Growing up parentless, we were never taught to love ourselves. We had no identity, no protection, no peace. Most days, we learned to dislike each other and fight each other. We didn't realize we all had one thing in common—that we were taken from our families or didn't have a family. That was the time that we should have made our own family within the group home. But because of trauma with us all, we directed our pain toward each other. I fought a lot in the group home due to how I looked. They thought that I thought I was better than them. I dealt with jealousy a lot as a child and adult, and to this day I don't understand that spirit at all. I focused on staying in school, at least getting my high school diploma. I was very active at school, being in sports and on the pompom team. I never thought I was better than anyone. I had too many traumas to the brain to focus on pettiness. I had low self-esteem. I thought I was ugly. I kept myself busy and active to have mental peace, as an adult as well. I had to defend myself for many things growing up. Eventually, me defending myself would bring on a series of problems in my adulthood. All we did was fight each other due to the trauma within ourselves. My defensiveness was nothing personal toward anyone. I had been doing it for so long, my soul/body would go into auto-protection. I didn't realize it. I have asked people to forgive if that ever happened, but people still take offense.

When trauma becomes your norm, you start believing that it is what it is, and that this is what you deserve. So by the time I reached my adult life, everything was buried in my subconscious, but it influenced my actions and feelings without me knowing it. Well, I got married: more trauma, more neglect, more abandonment. I was abused physically, financially, and mentally. I never have been a materialistic kind of girl, ever; the depths of me want to be loved by my husband, and I did not get it. I accepted what was given out to me, not knowing that it was a form of domestic violence that lasted for almost 20 years. I got married again; the demon that came with my second marriage was seven times greater than the first marriage. That marriage lasted for three years. It almost took me out completely during that time. I was seeking help; I was being attacked by a few leaders with their accusations. Being accused by leaders who were supposed to help deliver or heal me was worse in some cases. It was so bad I literally wanted to stab someone. My trauma was getting the best of me and exposing itself to me.

I was being hit left and right. I was homeless at the age of 48 and trying to defend myself from the lies of people who didn't understand my suffering. They didn't understand the depth of my trauma. Also, during this time, I temporarily gave up on God, I had some serious trust issues with Him. He was not my father. He was just God in my eyes. I was in my 40s, my life was falling apart, and my worst nightmare had happened: I was homeless for years, with nowhere to go. The life of an orphan, fatherless or motherless, is a painful journey.

James 1:27, TPT states, ***"True spirituality that is pure in the eyes of our Father God is to make a difference in the lives of the orphans, and widows in their troubles, and to refuse to be corrupted by the world's values."*** I really don't think that most people understand how important this verse is to our Father in heaven. Many are passionately chasing after the work of God, but the God of the work is concerned!! Many have a passion and desire for ministry, which God loves, but don't get lost chasing after the wrong passion; I'm guilty also. I found out during my suffering,

He has given me a passion for the broken-hearted, the captive, and orphans. Orphans and widows are mentioned 76 times in the word of God.

The life of an orphan, aka foster child, is not easy. You can't just say get over it, move on. Taking care of orphans is not a temporary compassion; it's beyond that. It's not just giving food or clothing. The mental compassion is what is needed more than anything. Orphans need to be taken care of, looked after, provided for mentally and physically. Both are very important, especially the mental part, with the implication of continuous responsibility.

I didn't understand why I needed to know about the orphans in such depth, but I found out that I am an orphan and fully grown. Why does that matter now? I just want to be loved by anyone—my mental needs to be loved by someone. But the word "orphan" would not go away from my mind. A few years later the Holy Spirit had been equipping me over the years for such a time as this, to take a stand for the orphans of America, and not just for orphans, but the broken-hearted and captive. He has given me a path to journey down which was very painful, to train me in a great capacity to heal and deliver the captive. The word stated in Isaiah 55:8: *"For my thoughts are not your thoughts, neither are your ways my ways, saith the Lord."* That being said, our earthly mind is shaped in what man says, how our life should go, and we have our thoughts of how our lives should go. But before we were conceived, God ordained purpose for our lives. Moses, Esther and David had some kind of trauma interruption in their childhood; all three bought great deliverance for their people. The greatest deliverer was Jesus. He went through great suffering for our sake. Some of us, in the same capacity, have gone through suffering to save a generation from destruction, from hell.

I dislike when people who have not walked in my shoes tell me or someone else to get over it. Baby boomers and some Generation X'ers that were born before 1973 had to suppress the trauma of the early 1960s. So our people of African American descent had to live with and get over hush-hush moments, and because of that, layers and layers of trauma are so deep within my people. The cover of pain, abuse, disappointment, and trust issues are so bad; it is so buried inside of many of us, it's time to stop saying get over it and help the individual to conquer the joy of the Lord; but before we can do that, we must deal with the suppressed trauma within us. The time is now to be set free and you can only be set free if you want to be set free. I know it's hard. I pressed for my healing and deliverance, I had to embrace my process to wholeness. I experience the real joy of the Lord now. I can't describe this feeling. Walking this journey, I never thought I could be delivered and set free from past trauma; layers and layers of generational layers, some subconscious, were suppressed within me.

You can be a 40-something-year-old woman, but in relationships, you are five years old because you are arrested in development at the moment of the trauma that took place in your life. We can be free in certain areas, but in other areas, we can be locked down in bondage. A lie from the pits of hell is *"what goes on in this house stays in this house."* The problem with that is, you are covering up the enemy's works. When you cover up the enemy's lies, they begin to grow and take root. When you have something that has taken root, it grows deeper, deeper, and deeper. Now you have many strongholds protecting the strongman. We can't hide the enemy in our homes; what we are doing is raising or training a child in the way they shall go, so when they grow up, they won't depart. So how are we training them up? In fear or authority? Sounds like fear to me.

Being in the foster care system, once they get what they need out of you, that's it. Don't think the system doesn't have a need for you. At a tender age, or as a teenager, they have a need, they have a purpose to gain, but once you reach that age of 18 or 21, the system drops you like a hot potato. Yep, without teaching you how to live life or how to have a healthy relationship. One of the biggest issues with the orphan is how to maintain relationships; because of trauma and trust issues, this is a problem. People who don't know how to handle a person with severe trauma, like the orphaned or broken, are so quick to tell them to get over it, or kick them to the curb. I didn't know I had deep trauma issues that were affecting me, especially in relationships, until my late 40s. I always had a pure heart with all people; my past trauma would sneak in without me realizing it, or I would become very defensive trying to protect my heart from pain.

Most orphans/broken-hearted, due to the trauma, really don't know how to live in this world. Some of our language or teachings (strongholds) are our insecurities, anxiety, crying, rejection, apprehension, fear, depression, social interaction, fatigue, intrusive thought, distorted self-image, risky behavior, self-harm, avoidance of interpersonal contact, loneliness, perfectionism, trust issues with everyone, including God—the list can go on and on.

I felt that I didn't deserve love, so I pushed good people away because of my lack of love within me that I did not get with family, friends and the opposite sex. I felt ugly most of my life. I was afraid to look in the mirror at myself because I was so disappointed in myself. The foster care system did not teach me how to be successful in life or in relationships. We live our lives as we know it, to be broken with a mask on. At least I did.

What are your first thoughts when you see a rebellious/broken youth or adult? My first thought is what happened to them for them to respond the way they do? As an orphan or a person with trauma, I find that we make up our own policies, rules and regulations to survive. But the average person would not know that because we as people focus on the offense.

For those who are orphan in nature, or have experienced childhood trauma, life still goes on. If you are reading my story, there is still hope. Yes, the system drops us like a hot potato; yes, I was a hard case so many gave up on me because they didn't know the depths of my trauma. I did not know the depths of my trauma, and mentally some can't handle it. For my mental state, I have learned to forgive them and move on. There are people in the earth that God has given them the capacity to handle me with care. It's the ones we overlook that have the capacity to push, care for you, heal and deliver you. God used those overlooked people to set me free. That's why I never judge a person by surface.

I'm still connected to some of my foster sisters. We all have one thing in common, that is relationship issues. Some have turned to drugs or alcohol to reason with their demons. We are so used to doing things for ourselves for so long, self-righteousness tells us that no one can tell us anything. They weren't there to help me when I reached out to them. I'm giving you an example of the mindset of most adult foster children (orphans). Not all are orphaned, most of the foster children's parents are still alive.

Satan, you can have your demons back; Jehovah-nissi is The Lord our Refuge. Your attempts to destroy us are dismissed; *poof,* be gone. Jesus paid it all for me and the others who have been traumatized. We have hope.

Our Father is relational. It is so important for us to get it right in this area: We all are family according to His word. He didn't mention to take care of the orphan and widow 72 times just to be adding words to His word. He knew we would be the weaker vessel in the earth, and I see it clearly now. This group needs lots of unlearned mindset, healing, patience, mercy, and grace. We need to know what love is. If there's no one to show us, we try to figure it out on our own and most of the time when we're figuring it out on our own, we are fighting abusive people that we attract because we don't know better. For some of us what we saw as children is our reality in our life.

But I'm here to say, if I can help you catch it at an early age or if you are still stuck, after 40 there is still hope—that is, if you want hope. Arrested development is real for that five-year-old girl that is stuck in an over 40 body. I decided to live when I turned 50 years old. I decided that I was not taking my five-year-old self into the next half of my life. I do understand it was no fault of mine that my life started like a tornado that didn't want to give up until it destroyed me. This can be truth for those who need deliverance from the orphan spirit as well. We can be delivered from arrested development due to the fact we thought no one cared for us, that we were mishandled, or abandoned by our parents, or they died and no one was there to love us the way we needed to be loved.

One of Jesus' names is wonderful counselor. God, my Lord and Savior, had a plan for my life, and he would not give up on me. We can give up on ourselves but know that God will never give up on you, especially if you choose life, and if you choose life, trust me, he's there during your pain or disappointment, your trauma of the past, the lies/accusations, and don't trust anyone else's attitude. Jesus sees your tears. Jesus paid the price for your soul, your peace, healing, and joy. Cash in on it. There were times I literally felt demons and angels fighting for my soul. I'm here to tell you, the joy I have is unexplainable. Nothing moves me anymore.

My wonderful counselors bought life back to my soul—Father, Son and Holy Spirit; it was not man at all. I surrendered everything in me to the will of God for my life. I began talking to the Father like a child about all my concerns and issues, and who was causing me hurt and pain. I also approached my heavenly father by letting Him know that I couldn't continue to serve Him in this broken place of pain. I was unstable and I needed Him to take care of my enemies. I started to see instant results, in less than 24 hours of bringing my concerns to Him. I make it my business now to bring everything to Him. I have so much joy now. The Bible says, "The joy of the Lord is my strength." That is so true in my case; for the first time in my life, life doesn't have me, I have life with its abundance.

I speak to the over 40-year-olds, trapped in arrested development, that have a five-year-old mind. Come on out, little girl, come on out. There's still hope after 40; there is hope at 21, 30, 40, 50, 60. Trust someone who has walked the journey. Allow Jesus to heal her. When everyone else gives up because the trauma is so deep, Jesus will never forsake you. Do understand, if they have never walked that walk, they wouldn't know how to begin the healing process with you. In a few cases some do, but most don't because most people did not have to walk the walk of an orphan, which is a totally different trauma than the average trauma.

See, every trauma, suffering and trial that I had to experience was for the greater glory. After 49 years, I finally see that all things did work out for my good. God has raised me up to understand trauma of many kinds, to give grace and mercy to the broken-hearted and to set the captives free. I have the patience for you because this new journey just began for me. Yes, I am over 50 but I conquered. I realize this process I had to push through was for a generation who is living in a system of trauma and those who live in the realm of the orphan spirit. When you are called and anointed it does not matter how many setbacks you have, Jesus called you. You're called to come with spoken promises attached to your life. There is hope, regardless of your age. What the devil meant for bad God will turn around for your good. I have two Bible scriptures that will help you during your process, Romans 8 and Psalms 139. These chapters let me know that I mattered and that God loves and sees everything concerning me. Just like surgery, the healing process takes time and comes with instructions. It is the same in the spiritual realm. Embrace the process.

I was born, my life was turned upside down and now I am ready to conquer for the Kingdom of God and the broken-hearted.

Native of Detroit, Michigan, Elder Sabrina Renee Penn started her spiritual journey at the age of 27. She was spiritually nurtured and groomed under the leadership of Pastor Leon and Jacqueline Jones of Renewed Hope Christian Worship Center (previously known as Imani Community Center). There she was ordained as a licensed minister.

In May 2015, Penn transitioned to New Covenant Life Ministry under the leadership of Bishop Randolph and Overseer Tanya Adams. There she serves as an ordained Elder, the Chief Administrator and Financial Director.

Penn is the CEO of Amazing Graces Foundation, Inc. - a non-profit organization that provides sponsorships to individuals in need.

SURVIVING BEYOND THE SHAME

Elder Sabrina Renee Penn

Manage to keep moving forward farther than the normal length of progress even when you are bound by feelings of unworthiness, distress and/or humiliation. Keep showing up and exceed past your thoughts, feelings, and imaginations of yourself.

As I sit here thinking about my life, several memories come to mind. One thought is how our parents used to say "SHAME ON YOU" when we did something of which they did not approve. Wow, how that statement has scared so many of us in our life's journey. See, this statement is a negative announcement over your life and puts you in spiritual jail, making you feel that you are not worthy because of what you did based on your decisions. But what do you do when you are faced with a situation that was forced on you and caused you to have feelings of shame? How do you get rid of the innermost feeling(s) that fester within the pit of your soul? Well, I will share my story about the **pain, process, purpose, promise, and peace** concerning shame.

The Pain

At nine years old, I was a victim of sexual, mental, emotional, and physical abuse. I could never understand how a person who was supposed to protect you could do such a horrific thing to a child. I was told if I told anyone, they would die, and I believed it. The fear that I felt surpassed the physical pain that moved throughout my little body. I can still hear those words right now: "If you love me, you will do this for me." What does love have to do with abuse? I thought love was not supposed to hurt. Then to top it off, other words were said: "If you don't do what I said, it will be your fault that others will get hurt." Oh no, now it's my fault that people will be hurt according to my immature young mind. How was I supposed to process all that was whispered in my ears every time the incidents happened? Here is where the shame began for me. I felt dirty, nasty, unworthy, ugly and most of all, extremely disgusted.

Being the only girl living in a three-bedroom apartment in the projects was extremely hard for me. Why? Because there were nine boys living there too, who had a field day teasing me. As a little girl, I was very tall and shapely for my age and my brothers and cousins used to tease me terribly about my physical build. I did not have anyone to fight for me or to protect me, so I would just cry. I would try to go off to my room and hide, but they would follow me. Man, this walk down memory lane is triggering some emotions I thought I had dealt with, but instead I see now that I have just buried them. In addition, with the feelings of shame and fear, I know now that I began to feel anger, bitterness, hatred and loneliness. However, as a nine-year-old little girl, I did not have any idea what to do with all those emotions, so I would isolate myself, sit and rock in a chair and have an introspection moment.

This is when you think about your own actions or inner thoughts without voicing your feelings outward. I was even mad at myself because my body was reacting to actions that I hated, and I could not make it stop. I felt like my body had betrayed me and made the perpetrator think I liked what was done to me. What was a little girl supposed to do? I was silently screaming HELP ME!!! But there was no help anywhere in sight.

The Process

As I got older, I wanted to take control and secretly hurt everyone that hurt me. I wanted them all to feel all the shame, pain, and humiliation that I had to deal with because of what others had done to me. Now that I think about it, you can say I had an addiction to shame. According to Webster's dictionary, addiction means an unusually great interest in something or a need to do or have something. I wanted to control, to be validated, to be paid attention to, and to get revenge. During that time, that was my goal in life—at least that's what I thought. As I continued to walk the shameful journey in my life, what I thought was hurting all my offenders caused more shame to come upon me. I realized that for me to cover the very root of my pain that caused shame, I began diverting the pain by cutting myself. Yes, not only did I want to hurt others, but I also hurt myself on purpose. I did not like myself due to the multiple layers of shame that were growing inside me. I became promiscuous, a drunkard, addicted to prescription drugs (Librium and Valium), became a food addict and a marijuana smoker. The shame in my life caused me to think of myself as damaged goods. The enemy had my mind so messed up that I feared that my shameful incidents would be exposed. It made me feel unworthy to be loved, which pushed me into a place of isolation. I felt if no one saw me or heard from me, my shameful events would not be found out. I felt that the self-medication I was doing would stop the triggers causing me to have memory issues. I believed that the shame that was housed in my soul was who I really was. The enemy was out to steal my self-worth, kill my joy and destroy my mind. Understand this, shame is not a characteristic of the kingdom; it ties itself to your emotions, feelings, imagination and will and causes you to feel condemned. Jesus did not come to condemn you but to convict you to change. The Bible says, "Therefore there is now no condemnation [no guilty verdict, no punishment] for those who are in Christ Jesus [who believe in Him as personal Lord and Savior]." Romans 8:1, AMP. Realize that shame puts you, your mind and your body in a trap and binds you. It is time for you to decide to allow the Holy Spirit to dominate the whole you so that the roots of shame can eventually be severed, pulled up and destroyed by the Word of God. Is it easy to do this? No, however like anything else, if you feed it the right food and nutrients, the results will be a healthier you.

The Purpose

The purpose of shame is to make you direct your focus inward and view your entire self in a negative light. It causes feelings of guilt resulting from actions which you accepted responsibility for. How can that be if I was not the one who executed the actions that made me feel shameful? It was not my fault; I did not ask for nor deserve a life of shame, so why did I have to endure so much shame? I know it is not fair and someone needs to pay, right? Well, all those questions are legitimate but no reason to continue to live a miserable life. You need to make up in your mind that you must stop the actions and feelings of shame before they stop you from having an abundant life. If you are not careful, you will start to operate in guilt and shame.

Let's take a commercial break right here, as my bishop would say. Guilt and shame are two different attributes. According to Webster, guilt is a feeling of responsibility for a perceived offense, real or imaginary. For example, guilt is sayings such *as I feel bad for what I have done* or *I made a big mistake that caused pain to others* or if I *had followed instructions, I would not have failed*. On the other side of shame are sayings such as *I feel bad about who I am* or *I am a big mistake*, or *I feel like a failure based on what people think of me*, which caused me to change what I think of myself. Shame caused me to feel suicidal, depressed, and to walk in low esteem. I suffered all these actions to the point I just wanted to die. I felt like I wouldn't be missed, no one cared, and I would be better off. Oh yes, I was saved. Shame does not discriminate. I can remember one day I was in my bedroom, and I was reading Revelation 21:1-4, NIV, which reads, "Then I saw a new heaven and a new earth, for the first heaven and the first earth had passed away, and there was no longer any sea. I saw the holy city, the new Jerusalem, coming down out of heaven from God, prepared as a bride beautifully dressed for her husband. And I heard a loud voice from the throne saying, look! God's dwelling place is now among the people, and he will dwell with them. They will be his people, and God himself will be with them and be their God. He will wipe every tear from their eyes. There will be no more death or mourning or crying or pain, for the old order of things had passed away." I thought that that scripture was my way out and I was ready to experience the new earth, so I decided that this was the day I was saying, *Goodbye world, I stay no longer with you; I am out*. Well, I tried ingesting prescription pills with liquor and cutting myself; however, it did not work. So I cried out to the Lord and begged

Him to take me to the new earth because I could not take my life at that time anymore, and the Holy Ghost said to me, "You will not die, for you have a job to do for me. I have need of you despite how you feel and what you think." In other words, "I shall not die, but live, and declare the works of the Lord." Psalms 118:17, KJV. Thank you, Jesus, for loving us enough to stop us in our tracks from destroying who he created and not what we created of ourselves in our minds.

The Promise

> *"Even if we feel guilty, God is greater than our feelings, and he knows everything."*
> *1 John 3:20 NLT*

On February 28, 1993, I was involved in a horrible fire at my parents' house. I was trapped in the upstairs bedroom because the door had melted and since the fire was an electrical fire, the flames were coming through the walls. With no way of escaping out the door, I had made a decision that I was not going to get stuck in that room and die; nope, I was not going out that way. The first thing I did was call the fire department and let them know I was stuck in the upper bedroom. It seemed like it took the fire department forever to get to me. So I decided that I was getting out of that room. I was 30 to 40 feet from the ground, but that did not matter. I knew I had to jump out of the bedroom window to escape. So I pushed the screen out of the window, climbed out of the window, held onto the window ledge and said, "God, if you are real, you need to show yourself now and save me from this fire." As I let go of the ledge, the most amazing thing happened. As I was falling, all I saw was white, like a bright light or like I was surrounded by clouds. I did not see any fire and I did not smell any smoke. What did happen was that I had an out-of-body experience. I saw myself cut my forehead on the steel basement door. What makes this so remarkable is that I should have fallen directly under the window down onto the basement steel doorsteps, but I did not. I landed to the right side of the back yard, next to the back door of the kitchen.

As I rolled over to sit up, I realized that I had split my forehead wide open and the blood was pouring down in my face. However, the most amazing thing happened: There was a voice talking to me. The voice was so clear it sounded like the person was sitting right next to me. The strange thing about the voice was that I had heard it before but did not know where it was coming from. As I sat on the ground bleeding, the voice said to me to take the snow that was beside me, pack my face, get up, jump over the fence with a broken knee, go through the neighbor's house, and get to the street where the ambulance was. Now you must understand that it was not snowing, but what I packed in my face was dirt and leaves, BUT GOD!!! He revealed himself to me. He let me know that I was not crazy, but He was the one who was talking to me through my years of abuse. He was with me when I did not understand, when I wanted to give up and check out. He was always with me.

Well, you ask, what does all of this have to do with shame? I lost my nephew in the fire that day and I felt if I had not screamed at him to go down the steps and go out the front door, he would still be alive today. His grandfather made me feel so bad that I lived and he died, and I felt as though it was my fault. Oh God, why would he allow me to live and allow a five-year-old to die? To me it was not fair. But the promises of God are true. For this scripture kept resonating in my spirit: "The Lord your God is with you wherever you go" Joshua 1:9, NIV. Everyone was telling me that it was not my fault and his parents kept assuring me that it was not my fault. I could not receive what they were saying and what God was saying. The shame had overtaken my spirit, my soul, my heart, and my mind. I felt like I did not deserve to live. Then one day as I was in a very dark, depressed state, God gave me a vision. As I was sitting on my bed staring out the window, I saw my nephew standing in the middle of a brick street and he kept calling my name. I turned around and began talking to him. I reached out to grab him and he said these words to me: "You cannot touch me right now because I just came back to let you know I am okay and I will see you later. I love you, Aunt Beanie." What an amazing God we serve. Even though I had been saved for 10 years, I was very sure that God was with me and his promises were true. I finally understood when the scripture says, "You keep track of all my sorrows. You have collected all my tears in your bottle. You have recorded each one in your book." Psalm 56:8, NLT. I was finally able to see God through my shame, suffering, and pain.

The Peace

> *Fear not; you will no longer live in shame. Don't be afraid; there is no more disgrace for you. You will no longer remember the shame of your youth and the sorrows of widowhood.*
> *Isaiah 54:4, NLT*

So let me share how you can survive beyond the shame and receive the peace that will allow you to continue to move forward in life. First, you must pray and pray and pray. Realize that the spirit of shame is a silent killer. Holding all that pain, agony and suffering will cause harm to your physical body (heart attack, headaches, high blood pressure, etc.) In addition, it will tear your spirit down (low self-esteem, unworthiness, etc.). The feelings of shame will not disappear like magic. They will gnaw within the very core of your soul. Will the feeling go away immediately after praying? NO! It is a process. You must be consistent in prayer for the Word of God to destroy those negative feelings. So don't ponder over it; pray over it. Second, you must make up your mind to speak to the shame. One of my famous sayings is, "When you get sick and tired of being sick and tired, only you can make the decision to change and just do it." Use your power and authority that God gave you since the beginning of time. Jesus is our example. When he was in the wilderness, the enemy tried to play with his mind. However, Jesus countered with the Word of God. So when your mind says you are disgusting; you pull that thought down and speak what God says about you. The Bible says, "We destroy every proud obstacle that keeps people from knowing God. We capture their rebellious thoughts and teach them to obey Christ." 2 Corinthians 10:5, NLT. Third, journal what are you are feeling. Write what you want God to know. See, journaling is not merely recording, keeping a log or diary. Writing your feelings and then seeing what God says about what you are feeling is a great stress reliever. Studying the Word will keep you more focused on what God says about you.

It was my pleasure sharing my story and I pray it has been an encouragement and a blessing to you. May the amazing grace of the Master, Jesus Christ, the extravagant love of God, and the intimate friendship of the Holy Ghost be with all of you (2 Corinthians 13:14).

Born and raised on the southside of Chicago, Evangelist Wenona Kelley has always had a passion to touch the lost, rejected, and forgotten. She began to encounter the power of God through extraordinary spiritual experiences beginning in her late teenage years, then while in active addiction to drugs and alcohol in the late 1990's.

Under the leadership of Dr. Matthew and Kamilah Stevenson, (All Nations Worship Assembly - Chicago), Kelley is an active member who serves as a leader in the evangelism ministry and on the outreach team. Kelley has impacted the lives of many!

Kelley is a natural mother to one and a grandmother to three. As an instrument to disciple, mentor, train and develop the people of God, Kelley is also a spiritual mother to many. Kelley is a published author, who believes beyond all intellect, that God can do anything!

UNBEGRIEVABLE!

Wenona Kelley

All I had ever known was a mother who lived right and ate right. No smoking, no drinking, no late-night partying that would deprive her of rest, and at a spry-footed, beautifully ripe 73 years old, she was still walking and bowling and serving, most of which continued in the middle of the 2020 pandemic. Mama was fine—and then she was sick.

I will never understand how it happened, but I would come to believe why as I replayed the last moment over and over again during the nine months following her transition.

At 7:12pm on December 11, 2020, I stood in her bedroom door and watched her exhale, in one breath, that which God had breathed into her nostrils seventy-three years prior. And just like that, her spirit flew away. In a desperate cry for what would have never been enough time, I screamed, 'WAIT A MINUTE!' but it was useless. I know my Mama would have come back if she could, if just to console her daughters so they could be at peace, but the Lord is omni-everything. He was, and He is, a multi-tasker. There was a date for my Mama to rest, and a day for me to grow up—in life, and in Him. He didn't have to do it like this, though!

You know you have lived and gotten older when you begin to experience the grief of bereavement closely and consistently. I have attended countless services, accumulated scores of obituaries over the last thirty years; even so, during the last four at the time of this publication, I found myself invited to either serve for, pray or extend words of comfort at, or was merely informed about a funeral two or three times a month. Those around would tease me about it, going as far as to say they didn't know if they wanted to remain a friend because all of my friends had funerals. Indeed, they all will, but the suddenness of my involvement in these environments was a proving ground for what would be a new testament of faith and relationship with God in my life.

From the very beginning of what would be the rest of my life without my mama physically present, I knew that I would be one who truly would not grieve as those who have no hope. I was not ignorant about that, but in all my hearing and reading of that passage of scripture, I had no clue as to what it entailed. At every final service I could remember attending, mourners, both believers and non, were inconsolable at best, hollering, screaming, fainting, knocking caskets over, and hollering 'NO!' as if it would somehow alter the truth of the matter. There is a people who are built to grieve uncommonly…with hope. In retrospect, I had begun to grieve as she lay for months preparing to leave life in this world. And so it was.

I had to become resolved with this new reality and seized the sorrow.

In doing so, I was able to actually experience bereavement by becoming a student to its lessons.

Whether it comes slowly or suddenly, grief grooms Grace in our remembering. Of course, I remembered my childhood and how I was raised. There were memories of vacations, incidents, punishments, my 'cornbread' whipping. (No eating after dinner or dessert and no going in my mama's kitchen after it was cleaned and closed for the evening! My sister and I got a lashing one morning because Mama forgot SHE ate the cornbread.) Nevertheless, the memories abound. In situations such as mine wherein I had six months of grief, new memories were made. Right here is where I encourage anyone caring for a 'terminally' ill relative to place under arrest the right to express the broken-heartedness. Be it. Feel it; just keep in mind that you have something to do both now and when that assignment is over. Live.

Seizing the sorrow for me came in the form of learning new things about Mama. These were revelations and insights, so late in the game it seemed, that not only gave me a clear understanding of how and why I am, but most fascinatingly, who my mama was! I had never really known her. In my grief I met my mama for the first time. It also meant becoming something I never aspired to be— never even considered it. Before I knew it, I was some form of a medical nurse. The fact that Mama needed tender care caused me to face some fears and angst. I hate needles, but there I was administering blood thinners and insulin. I have no medical training, but there I was adjusting, monitoring, and maintaining a feeding tube. I'm no muscle-bound woman, but there I was lifting and turning and pushing and pulling my mama, gingerly, to bathe and clean a body I had never seen. In hindsight, focusing on the tasks at which I had become skilled in order to ensure her comfort grew me in Grace through grief. The joy of The Lord MUST have been present because I felt a strength that was not my own. Good or bad, the heart doesn't lie. Deception starts in the mind. In my mind this couldn't be happening. It couldn't be true. But it was, and my heart knew it. After becoming a mother myself, for which I was certainly not ready, this was an execution of the second most significant task of a lifetime. Though it may seem strange, even in agonizing reflection of it all, I am grateful to have been the one. It was my awfully honorable duty.

In seasons of grief, more dies than your loved one. Something in you changes. After Mama's time on earth ended, my energy died. I felt weary and physically tired most of the time.

Some relationships died. Friends and family members alike are not always capable of handling how grief transmutes one's nature. It has a way of re-establishing the physiological makeup of the heart and brain. I know that notion is almost incomprehensible; nevertheless, my responses to ordinary and commonplace situations were changing. Grief was changing my attitude about some things. I cared more for some and less for others. Some things mattered. Some now did not. What had been my staunch position in areas of life that I believed were important to fight about and against were now revolutionized. I was being given, and subsequently extending, Grace and more Grace. The weight of this mission was expanding the core of compassion from which I am built. It became increasingly abundant toward others and me. That was new, but I soon recognized that not everyone is capable of adjusting to this form of rework. I was definitely not choosing this 'do over' of my own volition, but I was yet evolving. Everyone would not, and *could* not…stay.

I suffered consistent mental and emotional heart attacks. At times it felt like my own life had died. I was figuratively standing in a grave not ready for me. It was the loneliest loneliness ever.

Witnessing my mama die, for me, was 'unbegrievable.' I had to manage my moments.

Things I stubbornly kept around that had no evident use were a constant reminder and trigger to hopeless moments that turned into days, then weeks. I had to clean it up. Throw it out. This was not my removing all proof of Mama's existence. This was clearing out her accumulation of what she would never need again. It was clutter. What I kept was for the sake of posterity alone, so I would be able to move through the pain.

This management meant I had to have faith in something, and genuine people around who would not leave. "Lord Increase My Faith" was no longer just a church service offering time song. I was being built in believing something I had never seen, would keep comfort, and carry me through. With all that was about me, my faith was really all I had.

My belief that I had always been a good friend, notwithstanding, I found it critical to practice the biblical principle of showing oneself friendly at all costs, because the bereaved need real friends. At some point in this life, we will all make the special front row seating list staring at the lifeless body of a loved one. Be the few and the faithful...you will attract what you are.

The death-grieved will need patient friends, ones who will take their heartbreak seriously and truly love at all times.

My moments still happen. They just don't last as long. When I feel a stirring of emotion at the sound of Mama's voice in my head, or walk past her picture and the grief becomes new again, yes, I cry. Then I smile...laugh...BELIEVE...that she believed what she said when she lived, and what she sang in that hymn: "I dun died one time...and I ain't gon' die no more..."

That brings me joy. That gives me strength.

Those who acknowledge Christ as their savior die once indeed. They go from earth to rest, so why look for the living among the dead? We have always heard that people grieve differently, and my Bible says just that. What it does not do is give a list of ways to grieve. It gives one clear admonishment as to how we should that is different from how others will.

I am not in judgment toward those who grieve in despair. As a matter of fact, my prayer will be that whatever the act, action, or behavior one chooses to ease the gut-punch of grief works for them. As for me, I now actually *know* the Comforter, and I come with a message of hope:

You can grow away from the grave.

Those ideas and plans that do not make sense while you're hurting are not your own. They have been born of this circumstance. I kept thinking, *Why would you teach anything, build anything, write anything, be anything, help anyone, or go ANYwhere when your mama just died?* How long would I use that as an excuse to feel sorry for myself or manipulate others to move according to what I thought were my needs? I had to become one with this new normal and for me that meant doing those things that were in front of me to do; things I had some control over: hobbies, intentional rest and eating, and getting OUT OF THE HOUSE. My inability to move through this grief was apparent only when I used my own power. Lingering in the sorrow left me darn near suicidal! I felt at times that this was it, not willing to manage my moments because, again, Mama was gone, and my life was over, not appreciating the fact that a segment of her life was predestined to bear me and groom me so that I would have one too. That I know I didn't create myself or cause myself to be formed in her womb made my pity parties a drag. No one was showing up…not even me! I was being selfish and self-centered. These tantrums had to go if I would live out all that God thought of me before me…just like my mama.

Everything that has happened and will happen in your life has less to do with you and more with how your life will impact others. God has given me ways to memorialize Mama that will not allow me to stay at her grave. That little voice that keeps giving me new and next things that need to be done in, around, and through me has not gone silent.

During one of our chats before Mama left, I asked her, sobbing, "…but what am I supposed to do if you go?" She turned her face toward me, managed a grin, then answered, "The living gotta live. God got you…He got me too."

Accordingly, cry because you can. Grieve because you should… just don't do it in the dirt.

See you in your future!

Tanya Chenese Young, bestselling author, educator, and mentor, loves empowering, impacting and uplifting the lives of women and children. She desires to assist those traumatized from loss in healing spiritually and emotionally.

Her greatest challenge was taking the helm as interim pastor of Way of Life Christian Center, after her husband's, (Elder Larry D. Young) sudden, unexpected transition to eternity. God restored her joy through a healthy journey of grief.

Tanya's passion for education reflects in the success of those she has served for 32 years as teacher, facilitator, coach, assistant principal and principal. Retired, Tanya volunteers for Sherrod's Independent Mentoring Program (SIMP) Inc., and serves on various platforms to empower others.

She is pursuing her Doctor of Ministry in Biblical Counseling.

Tanya's affirmation: I lead, I serve, and I empower! "I can do all things through Christ who strengthens me!" (Philippians 4:13).

STORMY WEATHER

Tanya C. Young

> *When you pass through the waters, I will be with you;*
> *and through the rivers, they shall not overwhelm you;*
> *when you walk through fire you shall not be burned,*
> *and the flame shall not consume you.*
> *Isaiah 43:1-2, ESV*

Storm: a disturbance of the atmosphere marked by wind, usually by rain, snow, hail, sleet, and/or thunder and lightning. Stormy weather is unpredictable. It is characterized as tumultuous, disruptive and can be very destructive. Depending on the severity, stormy weather may be classified as a hurricane, tornado, blizzard, or tropical storm. Some regions of the continent experience monsoons and tsunamis.

Have you ever been in a storm? Not a regular rain shower! I am talking about the ones that sound like heaven is being remodeled! A storm so intense that the thunderclaps so loud your windows rattle and the booming sound of lightning makes your insides shake. When my daughter was a small child, she was terrified of these types of storms. She would get her blanket and sit very still, whispering, "The thunder lights, the thunder lights!"

I have personally experienced two devastating hurricanes in my lifetime that left nothing but destruction (flooding, buildings torn apart, families displaced and lives lost).

We all experience storms in our lives. At times, the waves of life come crashing and feel like they are overtaking us! Especially the storms that impact our finances, disrupt our careers, attack our health, and dismantle our families!

My aunt and I anxiously waited in the family area as mom was undergoing surgery—a hysterectomy, to be precise. As the surgeon entered, we rose and met her halfway. She removed her mask. "The surgery went well. Your mom is in recovery and slowly coming out of the anesthesia." She then stated that mom would be moved to a room on the Med-Surg floor and we could meet her there. We thanked God and the surgeon and returned to our seats, anticipating that we would see Mom soon. We continued to wait what seemed like an eternity. Each time a person came through the door or entered the room we both reacted. An hour passed and we became a little concerned. My aunt walked over to a telephone and she called back to what I believed was the nursing station, either in the ER or recovery. She was told that someone would be out to see us shortly. We continued to wait. Finally, a doctor came through the doors and called my name. Simultaneously Mom's doctor entered the waiting room from another door with her coat on. It was quite apparent that she had left the hospital and was now returning. Her body language was very concerning.

STORM CLOUDS ROLLING

They began to tell us that mom struggled to come out of the anesthesia.

WINDS BLOWING

Both doctors said that at one point she was non-responsive.

THUNDER CRASHING/LIGHTNING FLASHING

Then, like a well-rehearsed script, they tag-teamed to tell us that mom had and was currently suffering a major stroke—WHILE IN RECOVERY!

ATMOSPHERIC DISTURBANCE

My aunt, the nurse practitioner, immediately presented question after question after question: How did this happen? Was she being monitored closely? When was this noticed? Was tPA administered? The dialogue began to fade when I heard the doctor say that her lungs collapsed during intubation, she was on a ventilator and the stroke was STILL active!

The intensity of this storm impaired my hearing, just as if I was experiencing a hurricane, where at times I couldn't really tell what I was hearing. You think you hear a train when it's actually the sound of the wind's ferocity. I felt the rushing waters fall. I was going under as the conversation seemed distant in the midst of my storm's cacophony! My aunt grabbed me, and I fell in her arms. In the middle of the waiting room, we held onto each other and began to call on the name of Jesus.

Hear my cry, O God; attend unto my prayer.
From the end of the earth will I cry unto thee, when my heart
is overwhelmed: lead me to the rock that is higher than I.
Psalm 61: 1-2, KJV

THE AFTERMATH

A whirlwind of events spiraled from the date of the surgery. Mom was placed in ICU and her stroke continued to travel for over 24 hours. My aunt and I stayed at her bedside every minute of the day that we were allowed to, according to ICU rules.

Is anyone among you sick? Let them call the elders of the church to pray over them and anoint them with oil in the name of the Lord.
James 5:14, NIV

We began to gather community, including family, clergy, and friends. I contacted my pastor and the prayer team at my church.

The attending physician in the ICU was not able to explain why this happened. The hypothesis was that there may have been a blockage in an artery (the carotid Doppler test did not indicate that). Or maybe a piece of plaque could have broken off, traveled through the arteries to the brain, blocked blood vessels and caused the stroke. Neither one of these hypotheses could be proven. All test results were inconclusive. No one, not even the specialists, could determine what caused Mom's stroke. Mom spent weeks in the ICU. She would make small improvements and then regress.

> *Casting all your care upon him; for he careth for you.*
> *1 Peter 5:7, KJV*

There was no time to prepare for this storm. But like the strategies you internalize during an evacuation or severe weather drill, I intentionally sought strength from God. My hospital breaks were spent in the chapel making supplication and reminding myself, as I communicated with God, that I had no control of this situation. It was all in His hands. I praised Him, through tears, for His promises to always be with us. I repeated His promises of healing, miracles and restoration as reflected in Matthew 4:23, Jesus heals the sick and Luke 18:27, what is impossible for man is possible with God. I reminded myself that Psalm 71:20-21, NIV, declares, "Though you have made me see troubles, many and bitter, you will restore my life again; from the depths of the earth you will again bring me up. You will increase my honor and comfort me once again. We might be in the furnace of affliction right now."

There were so many reminders downloaded during prayer, including promises of peace, assurances of God's plan, and encouragement to trust him, no matter what it looked and felt like. My aunt and I showered my mom with love, intentionally with physical touch that she responded to. There were times when I'd get to the room and my aunt would be lying by her side, holding her, comforting her and reassuring her that she would be all right.

> *Who has believed our message and to whom has the arm of*
> *the LORD been revealed?*
> *Isaiah 53:1, NIV*

We spoke life over Mom every chance we got. However, the attending physician, who was later identified as an intern, repeatedly reminded us of the severe brain damage that the stroke had caused. We saw the x-rays early on. But he thought it necessary to say to us each and every time he spoke to us that a little over 50% of Mom's brain had been damaged and the expectation was that she would have "little to no quality of life, if she survived." He even had this conversation in the presence of Mom. This was his last time making that statement. I requested for him to be removed from Mom's case. The hospital honored my request.

> *Not only so, but we also glory in our sufferings, because we know that suffering produces perseverance; perseverance, character; and character, hope. And hope does not put us to shame, because God's love has been poured out into our hearts through the Holy Spirit, who has been given to us.*
> *Romans 5:3-5, NIV*

Over the course of two months, which seemed like an eternity, Mom began to make improvements. She was removed from the ventilator and transitioned to the Med-Surg floor at the same hospital. But she had a setback and had to be moved to ICU again. Family continued to hold each other up. I continued to hold fast to God's promises, knowing that he was in complete control of a situation that seemed totally out of control. I was blessed to have the additional support of my church family. At the time I was teaching. God gave me extreme favor with my principal, who provided flexibility in my schedule and support in making sure my students didn't miss a beat. There were long days and long nights, both in and out of the hospital. At times I felt completely overwhelmed. There were other days where I could barely assume a posture of gratitude, but I conversed with God, thanking him that my mom was still with us. Thanking him for the small increments of improvement that we could see, although there were no visible changes in her brain. She could not speak or move her right side. However, there were still notable improvements. She was alert, making eye contact during conversations. She responded to prayer and would cry when listening to worship music. She would hold my hand when I read God's word and His promises to her.

THE RELIEF

> *For our present troubles are small and won't last very long. Yet they produce for us a glory that vastly outweighs them and will last forever! So we don't look at the troubles we can see now; rather, we fix our gaze on things that cannot be seen. For the things we see now will soon be gone, but the things we cannot see will last forever.*
> *2 Corinthians 4:17-18, NLT*

In time, Mom reached several milestones. She was able to sit up, transition to a chair, with support, for short periods of time, and her tracheotomy was removed! This was major due to the potential risks of infection. She was still on a feeding tube. However, it was determined that Mom was ready to be moved to a rehabilitation facility. We sat with the social worker and medical team in one of our last family meetings at the hospital to plan her transition. My aunt worked with the social worker to find the best fit facility.

THE REBUILD

Douglas Miller wrote a song titled *My Soul Has Been Anchored*. Some storms are sudden and dissipate quickly. Some storms are unexpected and may last awhile. Sometimes the rebuilding process lasts longer than the actual storm.

> *When you pass through the waters, I will be with you, and through the rivers, they shall not overwhelm you; when you walk through fire you shall not be burned, and the flame shall not consume you.*
> *Isaiah 43:2, ESV*

Mom began her rehabilitation journey three months after the stroke. Expectations from the medical team were dismal. My family and I intentionally focused on trusting God as we went through this most difficult process. Although we were not prepared for the storm, our personal and corporate relationships with the Lord allowed us access to spiritual resources that were instrumental in keeping us focused.

This rebuilding process for Mom consisted of physical therapy, occupational therapy, and speech therapy. We continued to fortify and feed her spirit. Over the course of six months, Mom received these therapies. I also had to be trained as her primary caregiver. We went through periods where Mom plateaued in one area or another and had to be reevaluated many, many times. Therapeutic interventions were adjusted, dismissed, and/or reassigned. There were many times when the process became overwhelming. Mom became frustrated frequently and refused to cooperate.

How do you persevere, short term or long term, with assurance, joy, and peace in the midst?

It's very easy to find strategies on how to survive the external storms, hurricanes, tornadoes, tropical storms, hailstorms, etc. but information on how to survive the storms of life is harder to come by. The intensity, impact, destruction, and aftermath of external storms may also trigger internal storms in response. Whether you're grieving the loss of a best friend, or you have experienced the loss of a home due to a weather event, there are steps you can take to remain grounded so that you can survive and even thrive during difficult periods of life. The tornado that hit us as a result of Mom's stroke occurred over 19 years ago. The rebuilding and restructuring of life as we knew it started immediately. And even as of today I am still making readjustments because Mom has been in my personal care since I brought her home 10 months after the stroke. Her quality of life improved tremendously because God was and still is in control. Mom is not completely independent, but she rises every morning, makes her bed, picks out her outfit for the day, and takes care of her own hygiene with very little assistance (even with inconvenience). My mom has the neatest room in the house. Although she never regained her ability to speak or her ability to walk, she maintained her OCD! Every inch of her room, from the dresser drawers to the closet, remains consistently neat as a pin. Nothing is ever out of place. I have to be careful where I leave things in our common areas because she will put things where she believes they belong. Sometimes I can't find them! Mom will request cleaning supplies to dust her furniture when needed. She has developed her own means of communicating most of her needs. I would say 90% of the time we understand her requests.

In the spring of 2003, her one-year stroke anniversary, I had the desire to take Mom back to the hospital to visit the doctor who had very little hope in her regaining any quality of life. I so wanted him to see the miraculous! But I was unable to contact him. Mom can transition in and out of her wheelchair, she eats very well, and she participates in developing her daily menu. She loves ice cream, especially chocolate cones and butter pecan. It's still not clear what level of reading comprehension she has but she often chooses items to browse such as magazines and even books. She loves being read to and looks forward to daily scriptures. She has her favorite television shows, mostly cooking and food series. You better not touch her remote unless she asks you to! She also loves to watch her church live streaming. Mom will make requests to video call family, especially her sister, grandchildren, and great grandchildren. Occasionally I can get her to dance with me but that's not something that she loves to do. She enjoys gospel music and will occasionally request a song by Whitney Houston, her favorite R&B artist. You can always tell when she's feeling her best because as she prepares for her day, she sings *Amazing Grace*. Even with expressive aphasia you recognize the melody without a doubt.

This has not been an easy task. But God has fortified me for this assignment.

Many of us have access to resources and guidelines for surviving external storms. Organizations such as schools and businesses even conduct emergency drills to prepare for fire, tornadoes, earthquakes, etc. These external storms may cause trauma that results in internal storms. Whether you are facing an external storm or internal storm, there are strategies that you can implement to assist you in not only surviving but thriving in the storm.

Strategy 1
ASK THE LORD FOR HELP!

For some of us it is so easy to go to God on behalf of others. We have to remind ourselves that God is waiting to help us and answer our cries for help.

Hebrews 4:16, NIV: *Let us then approach God's throne of grace with confidence, so that we may receive mercy and find grace to help us in our time of need.*

Strategy 2
BE CAREFUL WHO SPEAKS INTO YOUR STORM.

During hard times, words can impact your emotions and cause you to see your situation through a lens of disparity. Never let your emotions/feelings be your compass, and immediately dismiss counsel (no matter who it is) that you *know* will be destructive or out of the will of God for your life.

Proverbs 12:18, NIV: *The words of the reckless pierce like swords, but the tongue of the wise brings healing.*

Strategy 3
YOU CONTROL YOUR EMOTIONS; DO NOT LET YOUR EMOTIONS CONTROL YOU!

During devastating times, emotions usually run high. When the pressure is on emotions can easily take control. Keep it together. It can be done! Remember, where your mind goes your emotions/

feelings and body will follow. You can choose to sink in the despair of the storm and stay there or you can obey Scripture and keep your heart and mind on the right things.

Proverbs 3:5-6, NIV: *Trust in the Lord with all your heart, and lean not on your own understanding; in all your ways submit to him, and he will make your paths straight.*

Strategy 4
KEEP LOVING

Love in the midst of the storm. Love helps you put the needs of others first and prevents selfishness or self-centeredness when the waves come crashing. Love promotes compassion, mercy and understanding. It causes you to do the right thing and even go the extra mile. Love helps you hang in there when everything in you wants to quit.

Ephesians 4:2, NIV: *Be completely humble and gentle; be patient, bearing with one another in love.*

Strategy 5
SEEK QUIETNESS AND PRAY

It's easy to be distracted by the noise produced by the storm (both external and internal). Draw closer to the Lord with prayer and know that His presence is near. Be still, God will comfort and provide for you. Spend quiet moments in your Bible. Allow God to fill you in these moments.

God will carry you through the storm. (Isaiah 43:2)

Strategy 6
WORSHIP

Sing psalms, hymns, and spiritual songs to the Lord. Exalt the heavenly father and communicate who He is and what He means to you. Read the scriptures that are associated with worship. Worship is a key that unlocks doors and invites the power of God in.

Ephesians 4:31-32, NIV: *Get rid of all bitterness, rage and anger, brawling and slander, along with every form of malice. Be kind and compassionate to one another, forgiving each other, just as in Christ God forgave you.*

Strategy 7
KEEP YOUR MIND <u>ABOVE</u> DESPAIR

Easier said than done, especially when your situation seems hopeless and all those around you are extremely negative. However, it *can* be done!

Philippians 4:8, KJV: *Finally, brethren, whatsoever things are true, whatsoever things are honest, whatsoever things are just, whatsoever things are pure, whatsoever things are lovely, whatsoever things are of good report; if there be any virtue, and if there be any praise, think on these things.*

1Peter 5:7, KJV: *Casting all your cares on Him; for He careth for you.*

Strategy 8
BELIEVE

Take the limits off God. Pray, trust him and believe. Even if the situation requires a miracle, believe. Sometimes when we pray for a miracle it doesn't happen. But sometimes we pray for a miracle and it happens. We have to rest in our knowledge that God knows best! We must be able to take the risk and believe that God will answer according to His will. He sees the big picture and knows the end of a thing before its conception. Build your confidence in knowing that when the storm is over, things will not be the same.

Hebrews 11:1, NIV: *Now faith is confidence in what we hope for and assurance about what we do not see.*

Strategy 9
BE THANKFUL

Find the blessings in the storm. Embrace encouragement and hope through positioning yourself in gratitude. Hold on to what God has done and look for signs of him working on your behalf. Remembering the times that God brought you through difficult spaces and dark places gives you confidence in knowing that you will get through your current storm. Intentionally give thanks for all things. Tell God that you are grateful for what He has done, is doing, and has promised to do on your behalf.

1Thessalonians 5:18, NIV: *Give thanks in all circumstances; for this is God's will for you in Christ Jesus.*

Life can be very hard, and at times it seems like there's one storm after another. Whether it be an illness, loss of life, toxic relationship, or many other things, life is full of stormy weather. The most important thing we must remember when going through these storms is God.

For over a decade and a half, Dr. Carleta Alston served as an assistant professor of English and Dean for Instruction before officially retiring. As the founder and CEO of Afresh Career Coaching, LLC, Alston uses her passion to help leaders build efficiency skills through strategic organizational development.

With her strong belief in purpose-driven living, Alston is the author of a book titled, 7 Principles of Breakthrough: Professional and Personal Growth.

Alston is a wife of 36 years, a mother of two adult sons, and a grandmother of a teenage grandson.

7 PRINCIPLES OF BREAKTHROUGH

Dr. Carleta Alston

Lunchtime in grade school was the worst. Anthony tortured the shy little girl every single day because she was not developing like the other girls. He slammed the palm of his hand on the table as he smeared imaginary circles representing the flatness of her chest. All the boys laughed out of their seats as the little girl shrank deep within hers. That little girl was me.

For years I battled with insecurity, low self-confidence, and simply needing the approval of others to feel validated. It wasn't until I turned 40 that I began to realize my inner strength. By the time I turned 50, I was well established in who God created. At 56, I can truly say I know who I am and whose I am. I have vision for what is next in my life because I exercised principles for my breakthrough. As I share the seven principles, you will be able to overcome stagnant places in your life. Journey with me through the "Seven Principles of Breakthrough," and I expect your life to change.

Principle 1: Commitment

How much are you going to be committed to whatever you decide to do?

Commitment causes a person to press through the breaking point. What is that breaking point? Simply stated, "the breaking point is the moment a person realizes that all means have been exhausted, and there is nothing else to be given. When you reach that point, push harder! Find that hidden energy to press beyond a strength you once knew until that greater force seems to come out of nowhere. It's in you, and you must call it into existence.

To commit to anything, first visualize the goal. Visualizing is the act of seeing the goal before you reach it. If you can see the finished product, it is easier to get to the finishing point. What do you visualize for yourself? What results are you looking for? When you can answer these questions, your commitment level increases and makes it possible to achieve the goal.

To achieve the goal in mind, finish what you start. There is absolutely no point in starting anything you don't intend to finish. It's debilitating. It robs your confidence. It whispers failure in your ear and in your soul. Don't be a victim of picking up hobbies and dropping them without seeing the benefit you were looking for in the end. Once you set a pattern of finishing one thing after another, it becomes natural to not accept incompletion. It becomes natural to want to see the goal manifested. It even has power to boost your morale.

When you take on the attitude of "never give up," you will begin to see a breakthrough of opportunities and success in your life.

Principle 2: Paying Attention

I am confident when I say, "It costs nothing to pay attention, but it can cost everything when you don't." Trails of signals and alerts are ever present, and it is critical to learn how to follow the signs. Signs speak to us and tell us when something is off kilter. It may be a physical response when you enter a room filled with tension. It can also be that intuition that kicks in when you are about to make a major decision and immediately pump the brakes because something did not feel right. These signs are guideposts meant for us to slow down and pay close attention.

The same is true when we decide to take a physical challenge. It seems as if the older we get, the more mentally ambitious we become, only to find that our bodies are out of alignment. We may have the will to do something strenuous, but our physical capacity is long gone. Here is where we must stop and listen to the signs our bodies give us. It can prevent injury, or worse, hospital care. Why is this important? Because paying attention promotes mindfulness. Being in tune with yourself, whether mentally, physically, or psychologically, is ultimately the way to prevent paying the cost.

The mindfulness I'm speaking about is driven by reflection. A stable habit of reflection gives attention to nuances that occur in our daily life that would have otherwise been overlooked. Reflection is taking time to meditate on a thought or action that crossed our mind at some point in the day. It requires spending time thinking about the meaning ascribed to the thought or act. It requires journaling those meanings for further reflection. It is a deep-level process of thinking. The more we pay attention to our surroundings, thoughts, and actions, the deeper we can go.

Moreover, reflection lends itself toward tracing our story. Each of us has a story that set the course for where we are today. That place may be good for some, but it can also be a pain point for others. The way to move beyond the pain point is to trace our past. Yes, it may bring forth unwanted memories, but it also brings forth answers and solutions. Until we can accept the decisions and choices we made from our past, we will remain in limbo about where we are going. It is through tracing our past that we remember pivotal moments where we turned left when we should have turned right. The end of the process is where we connect the dots. How many times have you told yourself, "I'm not going to do that again?" When we break through our story by paying careful attention to the details, we can capitalize on connecting what should have been done to what can be done right now.

Principle 3: Valuing You

Who are you, and what do you want? The answers to these questions lie within each of us, and at the root, we find value. The way we value ourselves heralds the level of importance we have in the "why" of our existence.

Value is not bought nor given away. It is an intrinsic part of who we are and what we think of ourselves. It is the level at which we love ourselves. A healthy value system carries weight and prominence wherever it appears. Have you ever noticed someone walk into a room—a board room even—and thought to yourself, *I've never seen authority and presence like that before*? It happens. People cross our paths all the time with confidence and charisma and to some –machismo. It is as if they figured out the mystery of life and walk boldly therein. Wouldn't you like to experience that type of confidence? Well, you can once you understand the importance of your "why."

Your value hinges upon your purpose for being on this earth, but to truly understand your purpose, you need to love yourself first. Not everyone struggles with the "loving yourself dilemma," but enough people do and need to know that it is okay to love yourself unconditionally. Learning to love and value yourself is the ultimate breakthrough. It opens pathways for you to be productive with your life.

When we make our choices in life count for something, we eliminate the spinning wheel that steals precious time that we could be productively building better relationships, better communication, better career choices, and an overall better life. So when you really understand the value of your life, you will experience the power of impact and influence on the lives of others.

Principle 4: Our Choice

Your breakthrough is just that—yours. No one can make it happen except you! Fear and intimidation are ever present when we are on a course toward growth. They are like two strong pillars that stand in the way of progress. Fear screams, "What are you trying to do?" It always makes the task appear more difficult than it really is. It is a masterful smoke screen that is unrelenting in its ability to mask the truth. It is not real. Likewise, intimidation venomously attacks self-worth, causing us to yield to the will of others. When we succumb to the will of others, we lose our identity. We lose our soul. This is real.

If we intend to successfully become our best selves, we will either stay the course and get our breakthrough or lose the battle. I'm betting you want to stay the course, and you are justified in doing so. There is no room for fear or intimidation when a person is striving to do better, make change, and grow.

No one promises an easy passage, but we will need to do it for ourselves. If we seek change to better our life, it must be change that we want and not because someone else wants something different for us. Let me be clear: It's our choice! Our hands are on the steering wheel. Our foot is on the gas pedal. We have the power to ignore the rear-view mirror and look straight ahead to our destiny. We own the breakthrough!

Principle 5: Nurtured Spirit

It is great to take care of our physical and mental wellbeing, but it is necessary to care for our spiritual wellbeing. To nurture our spirit is to find positivity in everyday life. So often the media depicts the worst in society, which leaves a crusted residue on our soul where we can spend endless days, weeks, months, and even years trying to scrub it away.

Spiritual wellbeing needs healthy relationships—ones that exhibit sensitivity. Our inner circle is a talisman for the types of relationships we accept. They are either good for us or harm us in ways that can take years to undo. Good relationships are marked by friends checking in on you from time to time, receiving support for any accomplishments earned, being a listening ear on the other end of the line, spending quality time together, and speaking an encouraging word during a trying time. These sensitivities are not forced; they are not mandated. They are born out of love for those we care about and want the best to be manifested for. They represent the external support that nurtures the spirit.

However, internal work needs to be done, and Christians know all too well that the spirit is always under attack. Chinese philosophers use the term "chi" to describe the internal life force. Whatever we believe that force must be reckoned with if we are to nurture the spirit man. If ignored, the spirit gets congested and polluted daily, requiring purging of bad thoughts, inappropriate actions, and misguided notions. It creates imbalance and confusion, if left unchecked. It holds us back from performing our best. It slows the process of progress. The best part about it is that it is not permanent.

Breaking through a congested spirit or bad "chi" can be eradicated through renewing our mindset. Growth mindset accepts the view that anything is possible and whatever happens to us is for a good reason. Seeking a growth mindset for understanding will reveal a better plan and a better way. These are the opportunities that replace negative thoughts. These are the opportunities that nurture our spirit.

Principle 6: Finding Inspiration

Nowadays, social media is the predominant locale for finding inspiration. Every single day millions of people scroll digital feeds, peering into the world of common individuals doing extraordinary things. With so many options, it is no wonder many of us are left wondering where we fit in. How can we be a proponent of change and inspiration like so many others have done before? To do this, we search for what inspires us. We lean into what comes naturally for us that benefits others. We act courageously to prevent fear from standing in the way. We let high motivation take control. Sometimes, though, that is just the beginning.

Finding the right associations can be inspiring. Connect with talented people that extend beyond your own abilities. They will help bring you up higher than where you are. That is growth. Break through the same peer circles year after year, with no change in sight, to avoid relegating yourself to a ho-hum lifestyle of regret. When we break through this sameness and seek outside the circle, we find different types of individuals. Diversity in relationship circles is critical to expressing a whole you. What we lack, we gain through relationships with others. I am not suggesting that we abandon existing relationships indefinitely—quite the opposite. Like-mindedness has its place, but it can never replace uniqueness.

It takes effort to hone in on your uniqueness. Part of that effort comes from exploring books written about extraordinary people. Reading biographies is extremely beneficial and inspiring. The stories that you learn from the lives of others motivate you to consider your own story and its place in history. As a society, we are increasingly inspired by movements that pull on our core values and arrest our natural plans to do something beyond the scope of our norm. By choosing to accept difference, we can make a difference.

Whatever inhibits you from embracing your uniqueness, lay it aside. It's dead weight. Freeing our God-given talents is a right, a privilege. It is something we are not to be afraid to display. The talent we have is entrusted to us to be that inspiration to others. It is an act of obedience to a higher power. Finding inspiration is our responsibility.

Principle 7: True Alignment

True alignment is finding that sweet spot where you know exactly who you are and who you are meant to be. For most, finding true alignment is thought to be almost impossible. Nonetheless, to know yourself is to be honest, transparent, and bold. Generally, when we think about the word honesty, we think about it in terms of coming clean and telling the truth. That's correct from one standpoint, but it goes deeper than that. Being honest with "self" means that we are not seeking external approval or validation; we are looking for self-approval and validation from a higher power. I approve of me first, and God validates me. It is a private matter where we get it right for ourselves. Honesty without transparency is void. When people are transparent, they open themselves up for others to see, judge, or criticize. However, it is a liberating quality that would otherwise be snuffed out. Therefore, transparency leads to boldness that empowers us with the ability to do anything we put our hearts and minds to because we are free. When we are free, we are in alignment with who we are, no matter what challenges we must overcome.

Another powerful tool for finding true alignment is meditation. Spending quality time meditating is not wasteful; on the contrary, it is necessary if we are to tap into a realm of clarity to guide us into true alignment. Whether we are religious, spirit-filled, or not, consecration is the pathway to meditation and ultimately true alignment. There are critical times in our lives when we need to separate from those around us for a season to devote to understanding our true selves. It eliminates distractions and causes us to channel our energy to awaken our spirit man.

It is a powerful tool in our alignment arsenal that should never be taken for granted or ignored. When you break through distractions, you will achieve true alignment, and the time spent consecrated and in meditation reveals true purpose, if you do the work and allow it. In the end, it leaves us in a healthier state of mind so that we can return to those circles as a contributor to the lives of others.

Conclusion

Each of the seven principles is a tool to grab hold of and use to break through the temptation to give up by staying committed. When attention is paid at the forefront, we break through faulty habits of dismissiveness. When we harness the value of our true selves with courage and tenacity, we break through low self-esteem and low self-worth. When we choose our own path, we break through giving in to the will of others for the sake of not wanting to offend. When we discover inner peace, we break through spiritual deprivation and spiritual bankruptcy. When we find inspiration, we break through depression, loneliness, and hopelessness. Finally, when we are truly aligned with purpose, we break through distractions and lack of focus.

The next time you are presented with an opportunity to be challenged, whether it is professionally or personally, don't be held hostage to the shame of your past when you can change the course of your future; don't be afraid, because you just might surprise yourself with breakthrough ability.

ABOUT THE VISIONARY AUTHOR

Dr. Monique, the Transitions Dr. is the CEO of Monique Flemings Enterprises a coaching and digital education firm serving faith-based professional women ready to unmuzzle their voice and create a platform for their brilliance. Her diverse background with over three decades as a physical therapist, minister of the gospel and educator, allows her to serve and transform women through a unique, yet practical perspective.

Dr. Monique is an international speaker, certified life-coach, six-time author, and six-time co-author, and most recently contributing author of two books with legendary Les Brown.

Dr. Monique is an unapologetic trailblazer for women of this generation and serial entrepreneur that has served as Director of

Clinical Education within her profession of Physical Therapy. Along with her other responsibilities, Dr. Flemings serves as the Director of Affiliate Churches for All Nations Collective an urban church planting organization. You can connect with Dr. Monique at www.moniqueflemings.net